Su-57

Russia's Fifth Generation 'Stealth' Fighter

Hugh Harkins

Copyright © 2021 Hugh Harkins FRAS, MIstP, MRAeS

All rights reserved.

ISBN: 1-903630-72-X
ISBN-13: 978-1-903630-72-3

Su-57

Russia's Fifth Generation 'Stealth' Fighter

© 2021 Hugh Harkins FRAS, MIstP, MRAeS

Published by Centurion Publishing
United Kingdom

ISBN 10: 1-903630-72-X
ISBN 13: 978-1-903630-72-3

This volume first published in 2021

The Author is identified as the copyright holder of this work under sections 77 and 78 of the Copyright Designs and Patents Act 1988

Cover design © Centurion Publishing & KDP

Page layout, concept and design © Centurion Publishing

All rights reserved. No part of this publication may be reproduced, stored in a retrieval system, transmitted in any form, or by any means, electronic, mechanical or photocopied, recorded or otherwise, without the written permission of the publisher

The Publisher and Author would like to thank all organisations and services for their assistance and contributions in the preparation of this volume – relative in-text citations are shown in parenthesis and italics: Central Hydrodynamic Institute, named after Z. E. Zhukovsky (*TsAGI*); Federal State Unitary Enterprise, Siberian Aeronautical Research Institute, S. A. Chaplygin; Federal State Unitary Enterprise 'State Research Centre of Aviation Systems' GosNIIAS (*GosNIIAS*); JSC Concern Radio-Electronic Technologies (*Kret*); JSC GosMKB Vympel (*Vympel MKB*); JSC KNIRTI KRRTI (Kaluga Research Radio Engineering Institute (*KNIRTI*); JSC NPP Polet Scientific and Production Enterprise (*NPP Polet*); JSC Sukhoi Design Bureau (Sukhoi Aviation Holding Company) (*Sukhoi*); JSC Tactical Missiles Corporation (*TMC*); JSC V. Tikhomirov NIIP Scientific Research Institute of Instrument Design, Zhukovsky (*Tikhomirov NIIP*); JSC Uspensky Avionica, Moscow Research and Production Complex; Komsomolsk-on-Amur Aircraft Production Association (*KnAAPO*); Komsomolsk-on-Amur Aviation Plant, named after Yu. A. Gagarin (*Knaaz*); Ministry of Defence of the Russian Federation (*MODRF*); NPO Saturn Research and Production Association (*NPO Saturn*); OJSC DMB (*OJSC DMB*); Rostec Corporation (*Rostec*); Russian Aircraft Corporation-MiG (*RAC MiG*); Scientific Production Enterprise NPP Zvezda (*NPP Zvezda*); State Research Centre of the Russian Federation; United Aircraft Corporation (*UAC*); United Engine Corporation (*UEC*); UMPO (Ufa-based Motor Building Association); Federal State Unitary Enterprise, All-Russian Scientific Research Institute of Aviation Materials, FSUE VIAM; Harkins, H. (2015) 'Sukhoi T-50 PAK FA, Russia's 5th Generation Stealth Fighter', Centurion Publishing, United Kingdom (*Harkins, 2015*); Harkins, H. (2016) 'MiG-35/D 'Fulcrum' F, Towards the Fifth Generation', Centurion Publishing, United Kingdom (*Harkins, 2016*); Harkins, H. (2019) 'Russia's Strategic Missile Carrier/Bomber Roadmap 2018-2040 - PAK DA, Tu-160M2, Tu-95MSM & Tu-22M3M', Centurion Publishing, United Kingdom (*Harkins, 2019a*), Harkins, H. (2019) 'Su-33, Russia's Carrier-Borne Strike Fighter', Centurion Publishing, United Kingdom (*Harkins, 2019*) and Harkins, H. (1996), Key Publishing *MiG Article 1.42/1.44* (*Harkins, 1996*)

CONTENTS

	Introduction	vii
1	*Mnogofunktsional'nyy Frontovoi Istrebitel* – Multifunctional Frontline Fighter	1
2	*Legikiy Frontovoi Istrebitel* – Light Frontline Fighter	19
3	*Perspektivniy Aviacionniy Complex Frontovoi Aviacii* – Perspective Aviation Complex for Frontline Aviation	31
4	Armament Systems	99
5	T-50 Flight Testing to Su-57 Serial Production	123
6	Glossary	193

INTRODUCTION

The Sukhoi Su-57 (T-50) was developed under the *Perspektivniy Aviacionniy Complex Frontovoi Aviacii* (Perspective Aviation Complex for Frontline Aviation) program to field a fifth generation multifunctional/multidimensional strike fighter for service with the Russia Federation Aerospace Forces from the third decade of the twenty first century. Taking to the air in January 2010, the T-50 prototype emerged from the LFI (*Legkiy Frontovoi Istrebitel* – Light Frontline Fighter) program that rose from the ashes of the cancelled Soviet era MFI (*Mnogofunktsional'nyy Frontovoi Istrebitel* – Multifunctional Frontline Fighter) program aimed at fielding a Sukhoi Su-27 heavy air superiority fighter replacement.

This volume, which builds upon and advances the work conducted on the 2015 volume, covers the Su-57 program from conception of the MFI and LFI programs from the early 1980's and 1990's, to flight testing of the T-50 development and pre-series aircraft and initial service deliveries of series aircraft to the Russian Aerospace Forces in December 2020. The Su-57/T-50 design is described in detail, as are its various advanced systems, including low-observable technologies, power plant, radio-electronic, optoelectronics, electronic warfare, navigation and weapons etc. All technical information concenring the aircraft, systems and weapons comes from designer/developer/operator documentation.

In regard to formal or informal writing, it has been deemed more appropriate to use the term 5th generation when referring to a specific aircraft design – Su-57 5th generation multifunctional fighter – and fifth generation when referring to overall programs – Russian fifth generation multifunctional fighter.

1

MNOGOFUNKTSIONAL'NYY FRONTOVOI ISTREBITEL – MULTIFUNCTIONAL FRONTLINE FIGHTER

The development road that would lead to the Sukhoi Su-57 (T-50) PAK FA (*Perspektivniy Aviacionniy Complex Frontovoi Aviacii* – Perspective Aviation Complex for Frontline Aviation) 5th Generation multifunctional (multidimensional) fighter aircraft was long and arduous, with many obstacles having to be overcome – political, technological and, not least, financial. The commencement of studies related to a Russian 5th generation fighter could be traced back to the Cold War Soviet Union of 1983, as the Soviet Air Forces were introducing to service the Mach 2.83 capable Mikoyan MiG-31 interceptor and the highly manoeuvrable MiG-29 and Sukhoi Su-27 4th generation fighter aircraft (Harkins, 2015).

In the mid-1980's, when the United States was denying the existence of the Lockheed F-117 Nighthawk (at that time dubbed the 'Stealth Fighter') and future advanced fighter programs that eventually emerged as the Lockheed YF-22 and Northrop YF-23 ATF (Advanced Tactical Fighter) demonstrators, speculation was rife that comparable programs were up and running in the Soviet Union. The emergence, in autumn 1987, of a recreational kit by American model manufacturer Testor, supposedly of a Soviet low-observable technology fighter aircraft carrying the spurious designation MiG-37, despite being entirely fictional, further fuelled reports of a Soviet stealth aircraft program designed to counter the American ATF. Testor had released the first model kit of the fabled Lockheed F-19, which was initially speculated to be the designation applied to what emerged as the Lockheed F-117 strike aircraft, the fictional F-19 model bearing no resemblance to the F-117 (Harkins, 2015 & Harkins, 1996).

As OKB A.I. Mikoyan was bringing the 4th generation MiG-31 long-range interceptor and MiG-29 frontal fighter to fruition in the 1980's, work commenced on a unified approach to develop a fifth generation multifunctional fighter (IFI) and a fifth generation lightweight fighter along with ambitious programs for hypersonic reconnaissance and strike aircraft (OKB Mikoyan). That such programs existed in the Soviet Union was disclosed in 1988 when the Mikoyan OKB Design Bureau

Chief Designer, General Anatoly Belsovet, revealed the existence of two advanced multi-functional fighter aircraft – Article 1.42 and Article 701 – (then under development by the bureau), although, in typical Soviet style, their existence would later be both denied and confirmed (Harkins, 2015 & Harkins, 1996).

In 2021, the Sukhoi Su-57 (T-50), which first flew in January 2010, was the end product of more than three decades of interrupted design/development work that could be traced back to the Soviet Union of the early 1980's. Sukhoi

Conceived following the initiation of fifth generation studies in 1983, the Mikoyan Design Bureau MFI (*Mnogofunktsional'nyy Frontovoi Istrebitel* – Multifunctional Frontline Fighter) entered full design. Construction of the first of two prototypes apparently commenced at Gorky (now Nizhny Novgorod) in 1986. The two prototypes, which were classified as technology demonstrators, received the designation Article 1.44, differing in some detail from the planned production variant designated Article 1.42. Fast taxi trials, according to Russian sources (unconfirmed), of the first of the two aircraft took place during 1994. It had originally been planned that the aircraft would be flown circa 1991, but technical problems, primarily focused on the power plant, along with political, funding and infrastructure problems, associated with the dissolution of the Soviet Union in December that year, all contributed to delays (Harkins, 2015 & Harkins, 1996).

The Mikoyan Article 701 is thought to have been designed as a long-range Mnogotselevoy *Perekhvatchik Istrebitel* (Multipurpose Interceptor Fighter) for service with the Soviet PVO (Air Defence Force). The two-crew concept was apparently a long tailless delta design with engine intakes for the two engines mounted above the fuselage and an internal weapons bay for the carriage of long range air to air missiles, both features enhancing low-observable qualities. It has been speculated that this aircraft would have incorporated engine thrust vector control to compensate for the lack of vertical control surfaces and would have been designed for long range/endurance to meet the demands of protecting the vast borders of the former Soviet Union. The break-up of that Union and the subsequent temporary thawing of East West relations, combined with the financial woes that befell Russia in the early 1990's, resulted in Project 701 being cancelled along with many other aircraft programs (Harkins, 2015 & Harkins, 1996). There was little known work conducted on a Mikoyan 5th generation lightweight fighter program.

The main driving force behind the Article 701 and Article 1.42 programs appear to have been to field fifth generation designs to supersede the MiG-31 interceptor (top) and Su-27S air superiority fighter (above). RAC MiG/Crown Copyright

The first Article 1.44 demonstrator, 01, in the Mikoyan experimental aircraft assembly shop, probably circa early 1990's.

In the immediate post-Soviet years of the early 1990's, speculation was abound that the new Russian Federation was continuing development of a fifth generation fighter design to counter the United States ATF program (the ATF led to production of the Lockheed Martin/Boeing F-22 Raptor 5th generation fighter that entered United States Air Force service in 2003). By the early 1990's, it was further speculated that the Article 1.42, then apparently claimed by the manufacturer to be in the same class as the four nation Eurofighter 2000 (later Eurofighter Typhoon) and the French Dassault Rafale, would have a comparable configuration, weight, dimensions and be designed to undertake similar roles to the Western European designs. However, the Russian design would emerge as a larger, in overall dimensions, and heavier machine than its European counterparts. A company brochure, released in 1993, suggested a tailless, twin vertical tail-plane, twin side by side mounted engine configuration. Earlier, unofficial, and ultimately inaccurate, artists impressions had shown an aircraft that closely resembled the F-22 configuration, but with slightly inward canted tail-fins. Around the mid-1990's, Mikoyan stated that the multi-role fighter was in the 35 tonne weight class and was a canard delta design, with large area foreplanes, leading edges commencing toward the rear of the cockpit section, and a fuselage of triangular cross section. Russian sources close to the program (unconfirmed) described the aircraft as being considerably larger than the MiG-29, stating that it was of similar dimensions to the Sukhoi Su-27 heavy air superiority fighter. Despite its large dimensions and mass, the aircraft was designed for outstanding manoeuvrability and kinetic performance, with a planned maximum speed in excess of 2800 km/h – several hundred km/h greater than its western analogues. High manoeuvrability would be achieved through a number of factors, including high thrust to weight ratio engines, aerodynamic configuration, which included no less than sixteen moving control surfaces, thrust vector control for the engine nozzles and an advanced FCS (Flight Control System) (Harkins, 2015 & Harkins, 1996).

It was speculated that a MiG-29 development had been involved in 1.42 program associated tests. Such assumptions emanated from reports in the early 1990s of a MiG-29 variant more advanced than the first generation MiG-29M. A company brochure released in 1993 revealed an aircraft featuring a new wing planform, increased span and a kinked trailing edge with no sweep on the inboard trailing edge, canard foreplanes with a notched leading edge on the wing-root extensions and, what appeared to be thrust vectoring engine nozzles. It is now known that MiG-29 design iterations were predominantly aimed at advancing the MiG-29 fighter series. Over the ensuing two decades many advanced variants of the MiG-29 (including second generation MiG-29M/K Unified Family) were developed outside of any fifth generation program (Harkins, 2016 & Harkins, 2015).

Page 5-6: The Article 1.44 demonstrator, 01, was built to test technologies planned for the production standard Article 1.42, which would have shared many aerodynamic characteristics with the 1.44. The Article 1.44 was designed for high performance, courtesy of two x AL-41 afterburning turbofan engines, intended to facilitate supersonic cruise flight in military power. Whilst the 1.44/1.42 was designed to outperform analogues in most parameters, high performance appeared to have come at the cost of reduced efficiency in the area of low observability. MODRF

When finally revealed to the world in January 1999, the Article 1.44 (as noted above, the two-prototype Article 1.42 technology demonstrator aircraft received the designation Article 1.44) emerged as an all-moving canard-delta with twin, widely spaced outwardly canted vertical tail fins (vindicating the authors' mid-1996 published statements to this effect, when the standard school of thought at that time was that the aircraft would feature inwardly canted vertical tails). It was revealed that the foreplanes, which featured a dogtooth at the leading edge, were intended not only as control surfaces, but also to generate a lift force when flying at high angles of attack. The design also had additional high lift devices incorporated in the large mid-mounted delta wing (which had a straight leading edge) in the shape of two leading edge flaps and a pair of large elevons. An unusual feature of the design was the incorporation of control surfaces located on the rear fuselage between the engines and tail booms, which apparently acted as rudder and elevator forces on the vertical tail fins, the former augmenting the rudders located on the outward canted vertical tail fins, which extend vertically beneath the wing plane. A large rectangular scoop-type air intake box was located under the nose section in a similar fashion to that seen on the British Aerospace (now BAE Systems) EAP (Experimental Aircraft Program) technology demonstrator that first flew in August 1986 (Harkins, 2015).

All of the aircraft control surfaces, including the vectoring engine nozzles, were controlled by the KSU-142 integrated control system/digital Fly-By-Wire FCS that was developed by the Moscow located Avionika bureau. The Mikoyan press release claimed that 'the wing, fuselage, control surfaces and vectored thrust –controlled by the KSU system – form a unified aerodynamic surface capable of adapting itself to all flight conditions.' The Article 1.44 demonstrator had no discernible air brake. It had been assumed, then confirmed in 1999, that extensive use of composite materials was incorporated in construction of the airframe. The Article 1.44 was equipped with a new design variable geometry ejection seat, which was more reclined than previous generation fighter aircraft seats, and, in a potential serial produced aircraft, the seat would be have been automatically adjusted in flight, depending on *g*-load. Like its western counterparts, pilots of the Russian aircraft would wear a new *G*-suit, although no details were released (Harkins, 2015).

In the mid-1990's, development of a new Phazotron radar system for the MFI, then stated to be designated Zhuk-PH or N014, was suffering from the lack of funding that had gripped most Russian defence programs at that time. Another radar complex apparently offered was a variant of the N011M passive phased-array then being developed for the Su-27M advanced development of the Su-27. As with the Su-27M, reports were abound that the Article 1.42 would incorporate a rear facing radar system for self-defence and an Optical Location System, the former being doubtful and the latter most likely (Harkins, 2015).

A new power plant, designated AL-41, was developed by Lyul'ka Saturn (NPO Saturn). This was a $4^{th}+$ to 5th generation engine, designed through utilising a three-dimensional computer model. The new engine, which would feature a digital engine control unit, would incorporate new advanced materials, including high load bearing titanium alloys and compacted heat resistant powder alloys for discs, shafts, and load-bearing body parts. Saturn claimed that a qualitatively new level of turbine-inlet temperature had been achieved with the AL-41 design, which apparently added some 250° centigrade to the temperature achieved in the AL-31F turbofan that powered the Su-27 family of combat aircraft. This increased value required new levels of technology for blade cooling, the high inlet temperature being required to allow the aircraft to supercruise (sustained cruise flight at supersonic speeds without the use of afterburner) at speed values well in advance of Mach 1. The engine logged a considerable amount of operational hours in various laboratories, meeting specification values for thrust, specific fuel consumption and acceleration.

Two-dimensional vectoring nozzles fitted to a Sukhoi T-10 development aircraft, T-10-16 LLPS. Sukhoi

The new engine design encountered a number of development difficulties, although, in the mid-1990's, Lyul'ka Saturn Chief Executive, Victor Chepkin, stated that the technical problems associated with the engine were over and that the engines installed in the first Article 1.44 technology demonstrator, which was shown to the Russian Defence Minister in June 1995, were development engines rather than experimental. It was stated that the engines, installed in the aircraft at Zhukovsky, featured circular vectoring nozzles – circular and box nozzle configurations were studied. Rival design house OKB Sukhoi Design Bureau was also studying thrust-vectoring engine nozzles for incorporation into the Su-27M and later Su-30MKI multifunctional fighter designs, with at least one Su-27UB utilised to test two-dimensional vectoring nozzles similar in function to those flown on the McDonnell Douglas (now Boeing) F-15 S/MTD (Short take-off/Manoeuvring Technology Demonstrator). The nozzles, which had a ±15° vector angle, were thought to have been designed for incorporation on potential series produced Su-27M aircraft, funding permitting – in the event the Su-27M program was cancelled in the early 2000's (Harkins, 2015).

In summer 1996, Sukhoi flew the Su-37MR fitted with two axisymmetric exhaust nozzles for the engines, providing vectoring in the pitch (up/down) plane. Sukhoi

By May 1995, one of the latest pre-production Su-27M development aircraft, code 711, had been fitted with two axisymmetric engine nozzles, although it was thought that thrust-vector control may only have been available in the pitch (up/down) plane as nozzle movement in the yaw (sideways) plane could risk damaging the tail-boom extending from between the engine bays. This was confirmed in mid-1996, when Lyul'ka Saturn unveiled a modified variant of the AL-31F, designated AL-37FU, Lyul'ka Saturn General Designer, Victor Chepkin, noting that this engine had ±20° vector control in the pitch plane only. Su-27M, 711 (re-designated as the Su-37MR) flew with the axisymmetric nozzles installed in April 1996, Sukhoi stating that thrust vector control as standard would allow increased manoeuvrability and improve take-off and landing performance. In mid-1996, Chepkin stated that Lyul'ka Saturn had a pitch/yaw nozzle 'in its pocket', and it was such a nozzle that was expected to be fitted on the Article 1.44 demonstrator as the aircraft did not feature a tail sting boom associated with the Su-27 family – the close side by side arrangement of the engines would obviously have had an effect on vector angle in the yaw plane (Harkins, 2015).

MAPO (Moscow Aircraft Production Association) – included Mikoyan from January 1996 – revealed that the Article 1.44 was designed for a maximum speed of Mach 2.35 (in excess of 2878 km/h). Supercruise capability was claimed to be Mach 1.4 to Mach 1.6, at which speeds, MAPO stated, the aircraft had a very long range. According to Anatoly Kvotchur, the test pilot then mooted to flight test the Article

1.44, the aircraft would have had a supersonic combat radius comparable to the Su-27S subsonic combat radius, indicating a supersonic combat radius in excess of 2250 km (Harkins, 2015).

This image of the Article 1.44 technology demonstrator displayed at the MAKS-2015 exhibition shows to advantage the under-fuselage air intake complex and the port side all-moving foreplane. MiG

A new first flight date had apparently been planned for 25 October 1994, although this also passed with the aircraft remaining firmly on the ground. As noted above, fast taxi trials of at least the first of the two Article 1.44 aircraft were reported to have been conducted during 1994, apparently December. In mid-1995, reports suggested that the prototype was undergoing further ground tests, including more high speed test runs, in preparation for an imminent maiden flight. However, it appeared that the financial crisis was so severe that that the development aircraft had not yet been fitted with flight-control system actuators, with reports of unaffordability of components required to complete the aircraft. Political problems became apparent, assuming truth in reports that the company was refused permission to fly, or at least display the aircraft statically at the Moscow show in August 1995. It may well have been hoped that bringing the aircraft out from behind closed doors would have raised its public profile with the knock-on effect of perhaps winning support from senior politicians, which, in turn could have translated into increased funding to facilitate completion of the prototype and the move to flight testing. Questions also began to surface as to the Russian Air Forces commitment to the project, and, indeed, if a fifth generation fighter with a take-off weight in the 30 plus tonne class could be afforded in the unfavourable financial climate then prevalent in Russia. Russian sources (unconfirmed) indicated that senior officers in the air force hierarchy were of the opinion that the Article 1.42 was too expensive, and that the service should abandon it and pursue a cheaper fifth generation fighter. If true, then this was perhaps the first seeds to be sown of what would eventually germinate into the LFI (*Legikiy Frontovoi Istrebitel* – Light Frontline Fighter) program that spawned the T-50/PAK FA/Su-57.

This grainy still shows the Article 1.44 demonstrator, 01, during its first flight on 29 February 2000.

The Article 1.44 remained firmly stuck on terra firma throughout the rest of the 1990's, eventually being publically unveiled, as noted above, in January 1999. At this time it was reported that MiG-MAPO planned to fly the aircraft in March that year. However, the long awaited maiden flight was further delayed, the aircraft finally lifting off the runway at Zhukovsky at 11.30 am on 29 February 2000, by which time the parent company had underwent another change, becoming an integral part of RSK. The flight duration was 18 minutes, during which the aircraft attained an altitude of 1000 m, a speed in excess of 500 km/h, whilst conducting two circuits of Zhukovsky with its undercarriage extended before coming in to land (Note: various reports state speeds as 500 km/h and 280 mph, but these values do not correspond with each other, therefore, either the km/h figure was lower or the mph figure was higher). Following the flight, RSK-MiG Chief Test Pilot, Vladimir Gorbunov stated: 'We all have been waiting for the first flight for so long, but it went through as an everyday event. The machine behaved well, but it is obvious by its handling qualities that it is a fundamentally new aircraft. So all the work lies ahead'. The second flight, which took place on 27 April 2000, lasted 22 minutes, during which the aircraft apparently attained a speed of around ~593 km/h and an altitude of ~1999 m, the undercarriage being retracted in flight (Harkins, 2015).

Ultimately the Article 1.42 program was doomed even before the Article 1.44 maiden flight. The Russian Federation Air Force was now looking for a more affordable alternative in the shape of the LFI program. The 1.42 program, after only two flights, was, therefore, quietly cancelled and slipped into the shadow of the smaller more economically palatable LFI program.

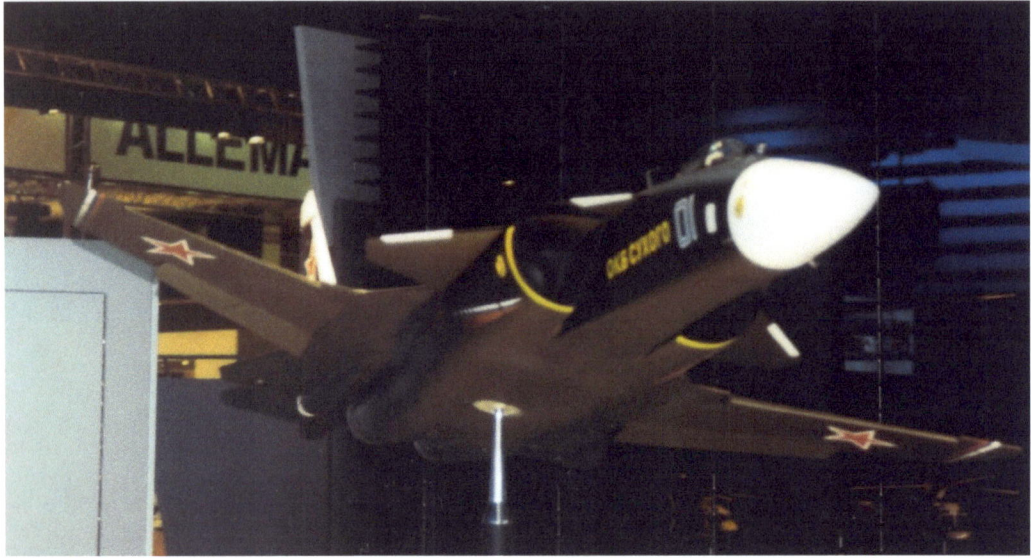

When details began to emerge of the Sukhoi S-37 it became clear that, unlike the Article 1.44, the aircraft was not designed for multi-Mach performance as evinced by the fixed geometry engine inlets, evident on this model of the aircraft. Author

While the Mikoyan MFI had always appeared to be the Soviet and later Russian Federation Air Force choice to meets its initial MFI requirement, the rival Sukhoi design bureau was also heavily involved in studies for a fifth generation MFI. Overshadowed on the political stage by the Article 1.42, in the immediate post-Soviet years the first indications of Sukhoi advances in potential fifth generation fighter designs came with the unveiling of the S-37 Berkut (Golden Eagle). Certainly the most outwardly radical of the Russian fighter aircraft designs to emerge in the 1990's, the S-37 forward swept wing design was touted as a Sukhoi offering to meet the Russian MFI requirement. The forward swept wing configuration had apparently been adopted by Sukhoi as a means of meeting the demanding requirement for 'super maneuverability' (the ability to maintain controllability at angles of attack in excess of 90°) at lower speeds, although this came at the cost of acceptable kinetic performance and supersonic manoeuvrability for an air superiority fighter (Harkins, 2015).

Forward swept wing flight research was itself not new. Prior to World War II there were a number of glider designs that featured forward sweep for the wings, and the National Advisory Committee for Aeronautics, Langley Memorial Aeronautical Laboratory in the United States conducted a degree of wind-tunnel work on the concept in 1931. In the closing months of World War II, Germany had conducted a number of flights with the Junkers Ju.287 V1 forward swept wing jet bomber prototype, which was flown for the first time in August 1944. This aircraft eventually accumulated a total of 17 flights before the end of the war in Europe in May 1945. The concept, however, was not successful, not least because the technology and materials did not then exist to construct a wing rigid enough to overcome bending and twisting forces without making the aircraft too heavy.

The EF-131 (Ju.287 V2 prototype) was almost complete when Russian forces overran the factory in 1945. This aircraft was then taken to the Soviet Union and completed where it flew for the first time in 1947 – 11 flights were conducted in Russia before work was discontinued. Attention then focused on a Soviet development, the EF-140U-1, which was abandoned in August 1949. Work now focused on a modification designated 140-R, which flew seven times before the program, along with the stillborn 140-B, was terminated in June 1950 (OJSC DMB). The forward swept wing concept, although not being abandoned altogether, then fell into abeyance for several decades.

This fuzzy image apparently shows a Soviet wind-tunnel model of a forward swept wing MiG-23 derivative employed to test the feasibility of forward swept wing flight in a high performance fighter aircraft design.

Like the Article 1.44, the Sukhoi S-37 was designed as a large fighter technology demonstrator, but the two designs took a very different approach, the latter's canard tri-plane forward swept wing layout apparent in this view of the aircraft. Sukhoi

When interest in forward swept wing research resumed in earnest in the Soviet Union around 1977, a number of scale models were evaluated in wind tunnels. Testing of a forward swept wing MiG-23 derivative model was conducted, and later forward swept wing models of the Su-27 were researched at SibNIA (now the Federal State Unitary Enterprise, Siberian Aeronautical Research Institute). Sukhoi also conducted forward swept wing research on at least one Su-9 and an experimental modification, apparently designated SYB-A, which was flown in 1982, a year prior to the American Grumman X-29 forward swept wing research aircraft (Harkins, 2015).

Sukhoi had apparently commenced work on the original S-37 program in 1983 (Note: the S-37 designation was formerly allocated to a single-engine lightweight multirole combat aircraft similar to the French twin-engine Dassault Rafale in size and layout. This design was cancelled in the early 1990's, the 1983 date more likely applying to this design and not the S-37 'Berkut' of the late 1990's, which apparently initially carried the designation S-32 (Harkins, 2015).

Development of Sukhoi fifth generation fighter designs were, like those of Mikoyan, severely hampered by the break-up of the Soviet Union, which was officially dissolved on 25 December 1991, this bestowing upon the program many difficulties, most damaging being a chronic lack of funding. In the immediate post-Soviet years, Sukhoi carried more favour in political circles than the rival Mikoyan design bureau, although this did not carry over to the S-37 program, which was more or less shunned by the Russian Federation Air Force. Sukhoi was in a better financial position to pursue new aircraft developments, facilitating construction of the S-37 – the aircraft conducted its maiden flight on 25 September 1997 (pilot, Igor Votintsev), whilst the Article 1.44 remained grounded (Harkins, 2015).

Top: The S-37 forward swept wing demonstrator. Bottom: Vortices stream from the wingtips of the S-37 as the aircraft manoeuvres during flight testing. Sukhoi

The Russian Federation Air Force to all intents and purposes shunned the S-37, unwilling to accept the compromise in reduced kinetic performance that came with the forward swept wing designs excellent low-speed manoeuvrability. Sukhoi

Design features of the S-37 included the forward swept wings with extensive use of carbon fibre composites in its construction, canard fore-planes, conventional horizontal tail planes and twin vertical tails, which were widely spaced as in the Su-27 series, but subtly canted outward. Sukhoi had previously adopted a canard-tri-plane configuration on the Su-27K (officially re-designated Su-33 in December 1998) naval variant of the Su-27, this being carried over to other variants, including the Su-27M, Su-34 and Su-30MKI series (Harkins, 2019 & Harkins, 2015). The canard tri-plane configuration had been demonstrated on the T-10-24, which effectively paved the way for the prototype Su-27K – the canards were incorporated partly as a counter to control problems encountered at very high angles of attack when conventional tail-planes lost much of their functionality. The S-37 was powered by two Aviadvigatel D-30F afterburning turbofan engines, providing excess power for high alpha maneuvering (Harkins, 2015).

Following the S-37 maiden flight, a limited flight program, consisting of a few additional flights, was conducted before the aircraft was grounded to allow modifications to be incorporated before flight testing resumed in spring 1998. By September that year the aircraft had conducted around 20 flights. By the time the aircraft was revealed to the public at the Moscow International Airshow in August 1999, the S-37 had conducted more than fifty flights. Following another grounding for maintenance, updates and an overhaul of its two D-30F engines, the aircraft, now designated Su-47, resumed flight testing in June 2001, by which time more than 100 flights had been conducted, including a number at supersonic speeds. Phase 1 of the flight test program was apparently completed in December 2001, the aircraft having conducted 149 flights since its maiden flight in September 1997. However, the Su-47 (S-37) was far from suitable as a 5th generation fighter, the Russian Federation Air Force now moving toward increased low-observable qualities incorporated in a smaller design than that of the large S-37 (Harkins, 2015).

The S-37 had emerged in the 1990's as Sukhoi studied advanced technologies with the potential to arrive at a lower cost alternative to the Article 1.42 MFI, the affordability of which was in question. However, as had been the case with the Article 1.42/1.44, the Su-47 (S-37) ultimately fell by the wayside as thinking turned towards a smaller, lighter fifth generation fighter design to be pursued under the LFI program. Whilst such a fifth generation fighter was being developed, it was necessary, in the face of growing obsolescence of the Russian tactical fighter aircraft fleet, to pursue 4th+/4th++ generation fighter designs in the mold of the Sukhoi Su-30SM multi-functional strike fighter, Sukhoi Su-35S multidimensional strike fighter and modernised RSK-MiG MiG-31BM multi-functional interceptor/strike fighters – all three entering service with the Russian Air Force (Aerospace Forces from 1 August 2015) from the first half of the second decade of the twenty first century. The MiG brand name continued with a line of 4th+/4th++ generation developments of the MiG-29 line, culminating with the MiG-35.

A model of the Su-47 was installed at the M.M. Gromov centre for the opening ceremony of the Alley of Heroes, August 2021. UAC

Top: With cancellation of the Article 701, the 4th generation MiG-31 continued to be run on in post-Cold War Russia, only in the twenty first century receiving substantial updates, allowing it to continue in service as a long-range interceptor in the shape of the 4th+ generation modernised MiG-31BM. Bottom: The Su-35S and Su-30SM – here operating with the Russian Knights aerobatic display team – entered service with the Russian Federation Air Force in 2014. RAC/Sukhoi

2

LEGIKIY FRONTOVOI ISTREBITEL – LIGHT FRONTLINE FIGHTER

In 1997, whilst the Article 1.44 MFI (Multifunctional Frontline Fighter) demonstrator remained firmly on the ground, MiG-MAPO had revealed that the company was conducting work on various single and twin engine designs for a lightweight fifth generation multifunctional fighter aircraft. The company drew on design work that had been conducted in the 1980's for a lightweight fighter to complement the larger (in overall dimensions), heavier MFI then under development in the shape of the Article 1.42. Among the studies conducted was a design that was basically a smaller, in overall dimensions and mass, single engine design similar in layout to the Article 1.42, but this project was terminated around 1985/86 as Mikoyan concentrated on developing the MFI heavy design. Early in 1997, MiG-MAPO director of strategic planning, Alexander Ageyev, had revealed the existence of a new fighter aircraft design being developed under the LFI (*Legikiy Frontovoi Istrebitel* – Light Frontline Fighter) program, design of which, it was understood, had commenced around late 1995 or early 1996. Around this time, a first flight for a prototype LFI, it was estimated, could take place around 2005 (Harkins, 2015).

As noted above, in the 1997 announcement, MiG-MAPO had revealed that it was working on single and twin-engine proposals for the emerging Russian Federation Air Force LFI requirement. At this time, the twin engine proposal, it was projected, would have engines in the 10 ton class, corresponding to a thrust to weight ratio of around 1.3:1, whilst the single engine design would have had a thrust to weight ratio of 1.1:1. The single-engine design had little support, and later in 1997, MiG-MAPO revealed that it was concentrating on twin engine designs, which were preferred by the Russian Federation Air Force.

Although little is known of the MiG-MAPO LFI design, it was stipulated that it should have a superior performance to any proposed new build variant of the existing MiG-29 or Su-27 designs, such as the MiG-35 or Su-27M – the former being an advanced variant of the MiG-29 and the latter an advanced variant of the Su-27. In 1997, there was much speculation that the MiG-35 designation was attributed to a design associated with the LFI program, however, this was flatly refuted by the then MiG-MAPO chairman, Anatoly Manuev, who emphatically stated that they were completely separate programs, this being borne out by the fact that the MiG-35 did indeed emerge as an advanced 4th+ generation variant of the Unified Family of later MiG-29 variants (Harkins, 2016 & Harkins, 2015).

As thinking turned towards a lighter fifth generation fighter in the late 1990's and early 2000's, such an aircraft seemed like a logical replacement for the Russian Federation Air Forces fleet of MiG-29 fighters that were starting to show their age. From 2009, the quasi-dilapidated MiG-29 fleet was supplemented by a small number of new-build MiG-29SMT multi-role fighters and two-seat updated MiG-29UB's. RAC

In the 1980's, Sukhoi, like the Mikoyan design house, had been working on advanced lightweight fighter aircraft designs to follow the MiG-29 in conjunction with the MFI Su-27 replacement. Among the lightweight fighter designs studied was a program designated S-37, which as recounted in the previous chapter, was confusingly re-used for the S-37 'Berkut' in the 1990's. As with Mikoyan's 1980's lightweight fighter designs, the original S-37 fell by the wayside as the curtain was coming down on the Soviet Union. However, Sukhoi, like MiG-MAPO, continued studies of lightweight fighter designs. In 1998, it emerged that the Russian Federation Air Force was urging both design houses to cooperate on an optimum fifth generation fighter design. According to Sukhoi General Director Mikhail Siminov, both companies were '… close to signing a cooperation agreement to coordinate their efforts in the development of an advanced fighter for the air force', although such negotiations were tenuous at best (Harkins, 2015). In the event, collaboration efforts would fall by the wayside and, in 1999, Sukhoi commenced work under the I-21 program for a unilateral advanced fifth generation fighter concept that could form the basis of a replacement for much of Russia's legacy Soviet era tactical fighter aircraft fleets. The previous year, the Russian Air Force had released a first draft formulation of what would become the terms of reference for a fifth generation tactical combat aircraft – refinements of the specification would be issued at later dates, taking then recent conflicts and technology advances into consideration.

In March 2001, it was announced that Russia was close to defining a fifth generation fighter. Russian Federation Air Force Commander, Colonel-General Anatoli Kornukov, apparently told the Russian military news agency that the new fighter would 'be of medium weight'. At that time it was looking like the aircraft would be designed by the Sukhoi design house and that it would enter the development phase in 2005, with a planned service entry in 2010-2015.

In 1996, details began to emerge of the S-54 light combat aircraft derivative of the original S-54 that was dropped from the Russian Advanced Jet Trainer competition in the early 1990's. Suggestions later began to emerge that such an aircraft, seen here in model form at Farnborough 1996 – initially intended for the export market – could be further developed to meet the emerging LFI requirement. Author

The LFI program was being pursued alongside two other programs – the lightweight all-weather attack aircraft program and a program for development of a strike aircraft for long range aviation to replace Russia's ageing bomber fleet. It was, at that time, thought that the former program, aimed at fielding a replacement for the Su-22 'Fitter' and the Su-25 'Frogfoot' ground attack aircraft, could be met by a combat enhanced variant of the Yakovlev Yak-130 advanced jet trainer. The new strike aircraft for long-range aviation could, it was thought, be met by the speculated T-60 bomber concept, which had been around for a while. However, the funds drought that was effecting so many programs in Russia apparently led to the T-60 program falling into abeyance in the mid-1990's – in 2021 Russia is still pursuing development of an advanced long-range bomber under the PAK DA (Perspective Aviation Complex for Long Range Aviation) program.

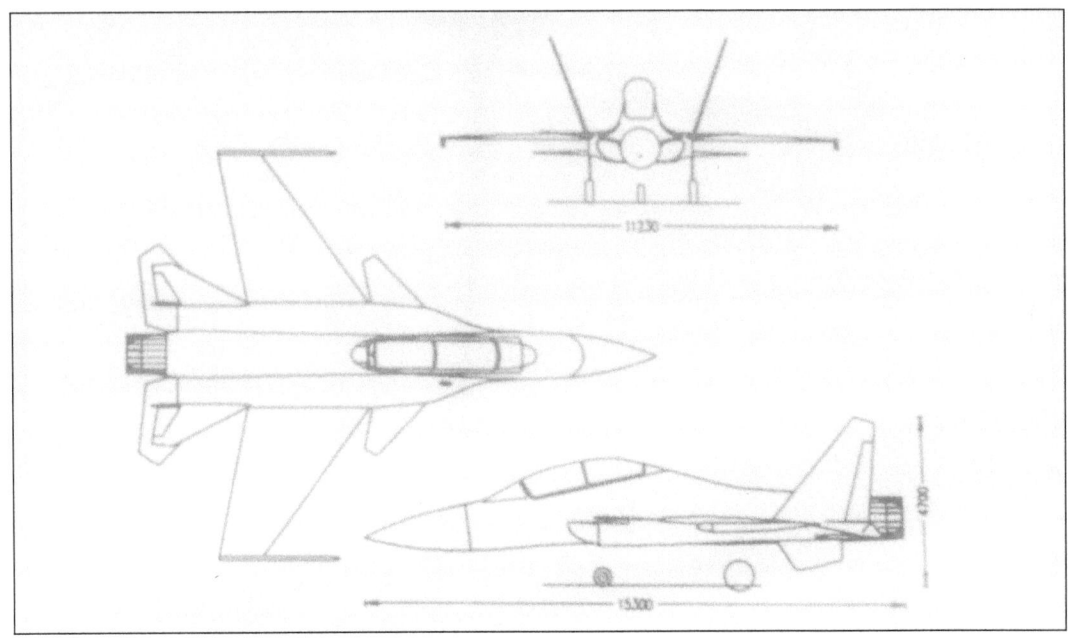

S-54 general arrangement displayed at the Sukhoi pavilion at Farnborough 96. While the aircraft shared many design characteristics with the larger Su-27 family it showed the Sukhoi switch to outward canted vertical tail fins that also characterized the S-37 (Su-47) demonstrator and the later T-50 (Su-57). Author

In early summer 2001, it emerged that the Russian Defence Ministry had issued a re-worked specification for its fifth generation fighter aircraft requirement, which now called for a 20 tonne class machine with a low radar signature, super manoeuvrability and the ability to supercruise (sustain supersonic cruise flight without recourse to the use of afterburner). Although the fifth generation fighter program was still being referred to as coming under the LFI program, as noted above, it was pointed out by the Russian Air Force commander that the design would be '…a medium weight aircraft, featuring extended multi-functionality against airborne and ground targets'. When the Russian Air Force released the new set of requirements, in May 2001, the I-21 Project was officially classed as an SFI (Medium (weight) Front-Line Fighter).

Once the new specification had been presented, thirteen companies/bureau/research centres, including Sukhoi Design Bureau, FSUE GosNIIAS (Federal State Unitary Enterprise 'State Research Centre of Aviation Systems'), NIIAT, Tekhnocomplex, TsAGI (Central Hydrodynamic Institute, named after Z.E. Zhukovsky), TsIAM and FSUE VIAM (All-Russian Scientific Research Institute of Aviation Materials), Lyul'ka Saturn (NPO Saturn Research and Production Association), avionics specialist Aerospace Equipment and Aviapribor and weapons developers Vympel and Zvezda-Strela, apparently signed a framework agreement outlining potential co-operation in respect of organisation and industrial matters of design of a new fighter aircraft. Funding was to be provided by the Russian Federation State, with additional funding to come from redirecting some of the profits from weapons export sales back to industry research and development. Further funding, it was hoped, would come from foreign investors in return for work-share and or technology transfer. By this time the power plant was expected to be a developed variant of the AL-41, development and testing of which was ongoing, with Lyul'ka Saturn apparently having achieved the requirement for 11 kg/kg thrust to weight ratio. At the time, there were other engine designs that could be considered, such as a development of the Klimov RD-33 that powered variants of the MiG-29 'Fulcrum'. Developed variants of this engine were then apparently producing thrusts of 9979-11793 kg.

Whilst Sukhoi remained coy about the proposed aircraft characteristics, speculation was abound that the aircraft would be in a similar class to the United States Joint Strike Fighter that emerged as the Lockheed Martin F-35 Lightning II. This seemed unlikely as an F-35 class aircraft was unsuited to the air superiority/air dominance role that would form the primary mission of the proposed Russian fifth generation fighter. By mid-2001, it was being speculated that the LFI would be based on Sukhoi technologies developed on the company's 4th generation Su-27 family, such the Su-30MKI/MKK, Su-27M, the experimental Su-47 (S-37) and the unbuilt S-54/55 lightweight fighter designs. Deputy Prime Minister Ilya Klebanov apparently indicated that he did not see a need for a competition between Sukhoi and RSK-MiG because 'no one else has similar technologies'. It was stated that RSK-MiG and Yakovlev could be given a degree of development work. However RSK-MiG rejected this thesis and applied to the Defence Ministry to compete in a tender, downplaying Sukhoi's stated technological advantage by pointing out that MiG had developed fifth generation technologies and had now flown the Article 1.44 technology demonstrator for the Article 1.42 project, designed to fill the now defunct MFI requirement (Harkins, 2015).

At around the same time it was being speculated that the Sukhoi LFI design could be based on the Sukhoi S-55, which was a single-seat multirole fighter variant of the developed S-54 that had emerged from the original S-54, which was dropped from the Russian Advanced Trainer competition. Such speculation, which had little credence, may have been viewed with a wry smile in some quarters as this unbuilt lightweight fighter aircraft was completely unsuitable for the long-range air superiority role, the main driving force behind any future fifth generation fighter for the Russian Federation Air Force. Projected performance figures released by Sukhoi for the 1996 S-54 light combat aircraft variant (as noted above this was a modified variant of the original S-54 advanced trainer submission) showed a maximum speed of 1200 km/h at sea level and 1650 km/h at altitude, with a ceiling of 18 km. The S-54/55 were designed for high agility with *g*-limits of +12/-3, and the aircraft had a design operational range of 820 km with a 3000 km ferry range (Sukhoi). While agility and operating ceiling were better than potential adversaries, range fell below that required, and maximum speed was woefully inadequate for the air superiority role. Primary sensor was to be the Sokol X-band multi-mission fire control radar, which had a stated detection range for an aircraft of 180 km in the forward hemisphere and 80 km in the rear hemisphere, although it is unclear what the typical RCS (Radar Cross Section) of the target was to arrive at such values. A possible alternative would have been a variation of the Zhuk-27 N011M, equipped with a passive phased-array antenna (Harkins, 2015).

The S-54 would have been equipped with the Sokol multi-mission airborne fire control radar. Author

Even with enhancements and weight reductions for the S-55 single-seat fighter variant, maximum speed would have been little improved, at best being on a par with the Lockheed Martin F-35 of several years later, which, being designed predominantly for the strike role, fell short in performance in comparison to modern air superiority fighters. On top of basic performance shortfalls the S-54/55 would have had insufficient load carrying ability and would have lacked any significant low-observable characteristics, although the designs small dimensions would in themselves have presented a low RCS (Harkins, 2015).

The 1996/1997 S-54/55 variants, which were conceived as lightweight fighter designs for the export market, adopted the canard tri-plane layout developed on a number of Su-27 variants (previously noted). Although outwardly appearing to be a smaller Su-27 derivative, there were many differences in layout, not least of which was the single-engine design, air intake configuration and outwardly canted vertical tails. In the S-55 lightweight fighter design the single AL-31F derivative engine would have incorporated thrust vector control, specifically a Lyul'ka Saturn L-100 vectoring nozzle featuring a stated 15° vector angle in the vertical plane and a slightly reduced vector angle in the horizontal plane. When unveiled, the L-100 design, which apparently added 60 kg to overall power plant mass, was intended for incorporation on to single-engine fighter aircraft, assumed to be the S-55 (Harkins, 2015).

This model, displayed at the La Bourget, Paris trade show in June 1997, was referred to as a single-seat variant of the S-54, also referred to as the S-55. Note the 54 code on

the nose. Author

There was no Russian domestic interest in either the S-54 or S-55 and neither type was seriously considered by any export customer. Larger more capable aircraft like the Su-30MKI/MK2 variants were more attractive as 4+ generation combat aircraft over the ensuing two decades, the smaller S-54/S-55 slipping into obscurity.

While the S-54/55 fell into obscurity, light combat aircraft variants of the Yakovlev Yak-130, selected by the Russian Federation Air Force to meet its advanced trainer aircraft requirement, emerged. However, these were mainly aimed at the export market and were completely unsuitable for the emerging LFI requirement, which specified a larger higher performance aircraft. Author

It was clear that any knew LFI design, be it a true lightweight or a medium weight fighter design, would benefit from a more powerful engine than the AL-31F powering the Su-27 family of combat aircraft. The obvious choice was a further development of the AL-41 developed for the MFI program. This new engine, designated AL-41F, was a smaller variant of the AL-41, unveiled by NPO Saturn in August 2001. This variant, to be primarily developed for a future LFI design, would incorporate design features allowing it to be fitted to existing or future members of the Su-27 family of combat aircraft, as would later be demonstrated with the 117S (AL-41F1-S) variant that powered the Su-35S 4^{th++} generation multifunctional/multidimensional fighter that entered service with the Russian Federation Air Force in 2014. Among the design requirements for the AL-41F1 was high thrust to weight ratio, allowing medium weight fighter aircraft so powered to have the potential for supercruise (Harkins, 2015).

In 2001, NPO Saturn Director, Victor Chepkin, stated 'we have done all the tests on this engine as a thrust maker', continuing, 'further work should be connected with an airframe, as the philosophy of the fifth generation fighter calls for control of the engine and thrust-vectoring system as part of an integrated flight control system.' At this time the AL-41F series engine was touted as having a thrust to weight ratio of 11:1, comparing favorably with the ~8.3:1 thrust to weight ratio of the AL-31F powering the Su-27.

The Su-35S 4th++ generation multidimensional fighter design, which entered service with the Russian Air Force in 2014, was the first operational platform powered by an AL-41F series engine – AL-41F1-S (117S). Rostec

RSK-MiG's argument for a state tender for the new fighter aircraft program eventually won over and, in September 2001, it emerged that such a process was likely to take place. A first flight for the new fighter, at this time, was estimated, somewhat optimistically considering the chronic lack of funding, for some time in 2006. By January 2002, the RSK-MiG, Sukhoi and Yakovlev design houses had submitted their various proposals to meet the requirement for the new fighter aircraft design, each heading their respective consortiums, which, in a number of cases, included the same companies vying for work on whatever design won. The anxiously awaited decision of the winner of the tender was postponed in March

2002, talks earlier in the month resulting in the Russian Federation Air Force agreeing to further feasibility studies to be conducted as funding was increasingly becoming an issue. Unrealistic previous estimates of US $1.5 billion for research & development, flight testing and paving the way for production, fell well short of the new estimates of more than $6 billion, the previous funding estimate now being relevant only for research and development. Around this time, it was thought that around 20-22% of funding would come from the Russian state, with in excess of another $1 billion coming from industry by re-directing some profits of sales back to research and development. Further funding was being sought from potential foreign investors, such as India.

As well as the design that would progress to development, a number of notional fifth generation designs emerged merely for aviation education purposes. MODRF

In April 2002, Sukhoi was authorised as lead-contractor to meet a Russian Federation Air Force requirement for a fifth generation fighter, kick starting detailed design work under chief designer Alexander Davidenko on what would become the T-50/PAK FA (*Perspektivniy Aviacionniy Complex Frontovoi Aviacii* – Perspective Aviation Complex for Frontline Aviation). This would build on previous work on fifth generation fighter designs, including work that commenced in earnest at TsAGI and Sukhoi Design Bureau in 1999, in regard to fifth generation fighter designs. From the start it was envisioned that such fifth generation tactical aircraft would take on the functions of a fighter/interceptor and strike aircraft, embracing a number of traits – highly efficient aerodynamic layout, excellent stability and control, incorporation of advanced control systems, new generation power plant, incorporation of advanced sensor/avionics, advanced weapon systems and significantly reduced visibility in the radio-electronic (radar) and thermal radiation (infrared) spectrums (TsAGI, 2019).

On announcing the winner of the competition, the Russian Minister for Science and Technologies, Ilya Klebanov, announced that Sukhoi would provide an initial proposal to develop the new fighter aircraft, at that time still being referred to as the LFI, along with a schedule for various development milestones, this to be provided by the end of 2002. Following its defeat in the tender process, RSK-MiG would have to rely on further refinements of its MiG-29 family of combat aircraft, which would lead to the new $4^{th}+/4^{th}++$ Unified Family of MiG-29K/KUB/M/M2/MiG-35/D. Yakovlev was now effectively out of the fighter design and building business, remaining within the combat aircraft design work with its Yak-130 advanced trainer/light combat aircraft (Harkins, 2015).

By late 2002, Sukhoi had completed a digital mock up of the fighter design and, by mid-2003, development was at the draft design stage, which was completed in the first half of 2004. In autumn that year, the preliminary design was submitted under chief designer Alexander Davidenko, this being approved for full development by the Russian Federation Air Force that December (UAC) from when the program would become referred to under as PAK FA acronym.

An early artist impression of the PAK FA. NPO Saturn

TsAGI work on the aerodynamic design included testing no less than 28 models of various aerodynamic configurations during the course of some 32,000 test runs. Work continued following the move to flight testing in order to confirm test results with actual flight data and refine those areas of the design deemed inadequate (TsAGI, 2019).

Whilst work progressed toward flight testing of a prototype of the T-50, ground based testing continued at a number of facilities on a multitude of development areas, such as fast sled trials for the ejection system, involving a full-scale mock-up of a representative forward fuselage/cockpit section.

At a news conference at the MAKS-2005 exhibition in summer 2005, Sukhoi stated that the program was progressing, with the Deputy Director General, Alexander Klementyev, stating that the Russian Federation Defence Ministry had approved the program. The technical design process was completed in 2006, paving the way for preparations for manufacture of the prototype, which commenced in 2007 at the Sukhoi KnAAPO (Komsomolsk-on-Amur Aircraft Production Association) facility at Komsomolsk-on-Amur. The test aircraft was assembled and delivered for testing of its aerodynamic form in 2009 (UAC).

3

PERSPEKTIVNIY AVIACIONNIY COMPLEX FRONTOVOI AVIACII – PERSPECTIVE AVIATION COMPLEX FOR FRONTLINE AVIATION

When the MFI (Multifunctional Frontline Fighter) program that spawned the Article 1.44 demonstrator aircraft fell by the wayside, emphasis shifted to a smaller, less expensive design to be developed under an the LFI (*Legikiy Frontovoi Istrebitel* – Light Frontline Fighter) program. This suggested a lightweight fighter, referred to as a Russian mirror of the American Lockheed Martin F-35 Lightning II. This was erroneous as the latter design, it was clear, would be inferior in conducting an air superiority/air dominance mission against a peer opponent. In the event, the new Russian fifth generation fighter emerged as a twin-engine design, larger than the F-35, but smaller, in overall dimensions, than the Sukhoi Su-27 family, and certainly lower in mass than the Lockheed Martin F-22 5th generation fighter (Harkins, 2015).

Eleven years after its maiden flight much of the Su-57 (T-50) PAK FA – Perspective Aviation Complex for Frontline Aviation) program remained shrouded in secrecy. It is clear, however, that the Su-57, which, despite being developed under the LFI epithet, emerged as a medium (specific developer documentation refers to the T-50 as a heavy multifunctional fighter) size fighter aircraft of overall smaller proportions than the $4^{th}++$ generation Su-35S, possessing the main traits expected to be embodied in a fifth generation air combat fighter. Notable fifth generation traits inherent in the Su-57 included: 1. Stealth (low-observable) characteristics – significantly reduced signature in the radar (radio-electronic), electromagnetic and thermal (infrared) radiation spectrums, along with reduced acoustic noise signature. 2. Multifunctional/highly integrated avionics/sensors, which in effect covered a range of areas relating to fusion of sensor data and sensor weapon interfacing to enhance attainment of mission objectives. 3. The ability to supercruise – sustain supersonic speed without recourse to the use of afterburner. 4. Super maneuverability, facilitated by a number of factors, not least of which was excellent aerodynamic shaping, highly efficient control surface design, incorporation of thrust-vector control for the engine exhaust nozzles and excess engine power (Harkins, 2015).

The Su-57 (T-50) was a compromise, incorporating advanced design features and technologies to arrive at a fifth generation fighter aircraft embodying stealth, supercruise, integrated management and super manoeuvrability. Sukhoi

By late 2013, Rostec Corporation was referring to a 'second-generation T-50' that would be fully equipped with integrated modular avionics developed by the Ryazan Instrument Plant. This variant would also incorporate the fifth generation engine then under development by UEC (United Engines Corporation) subsidiaries under the prospective engine program (Harkins, 2015).

Designing an aircraft for high performance at supersonic speeds, requiring high aerodynamic efficiency – lift and low drag – and endowed with super-manoeuvrability – retaining control during extreme low speed and high alpha maneuvering – whilst meeting fifth generation low observability requirements seemed at best contradictory, requiring compromise. However, Sukhoi, whilst having to compromise in many areas, arrived at an aircraft design comparable with other fifth generation fighter aircraft, certainly in the frontal hemisphere, for the low observability requirement, whilst outperforming all analogues in the super-manoeuvrability requirement and maximum velocity.

The expertise of TsAGI was prominent in the design of the outer lines/aerodynamic layout of the T-50. This included design of the air intake system, which had to ensure uninterrupted airflow to the engines in all flight regimes at subsonic and supersonic speeds, as well as meet the requirements for low weight and low observability. The design arrived at was statically unstable in both lateral and longitudinal channels – potential problems associated with flutter were satisfactorily countered. Low aircraft weight, around 24000 kg (this value apparently corresponds to loaded wright), was arrived at through a number of measures, not least of which was the extensive use of composite materials in construction (TsAGI).

Other bureau involved in design of the T-50 included FSUE GosNIIAS (Federal State Unitary Enterprise 'State Research Centre of Aviation Systems'), which had been responsible for design of the stand prototyping the Intergraph during the period 1997-2005. This involved development testing of various algorithms for incorporation into an operational T-50. During the same period GosNIIAS was involved in the concept development of the external design of the T-50 (GosNIIAS).

Previous page: T-50 aerodynamic model in a TsAGI wind-tunnel (top) and UAC diagram of the basic outer lines of the T-50 concept (bottom) – Russian language text basically translates to 'Generation 5 Heavy Multifunctional Fighter'. This page top: The T-50 employs a conventional undercarriage of two single main wheel units and a steerable twin nose-wheel unit. This page bottom: T-50-4 deploys its drogue brake parachute from the housing on top of the extended tail assembly. TsAGI/UAC/Sukhoi

The undercarriage system provided the T-50 (Su-57) with the required take-off and landing performance and, along with the specific excess power afforded by the high thrust of the engines, facilitated a measure of short take-off and landing capability. Knaaz/MODRF

In 2021, much of what was known of the T-50 (Su-57) design came from Sukhoi documentation released in 2012, and the subsequent release of basic specifications, along with what could be interpreted from visual observations of the prototype and first serial aircraft and occasional leaks of formerly classified data. Basic dimensions of the design included a length of 19.7 m; height, 5 m; wing span, 14 m and wing area, 82 m^2, very close to the respective values of 20 m (length), 14 m (wing span) and 4.8 m (height) estimated in the 2015 volume, published prior to the data being released.

The basic design incorporated a fuselage with 'dogtooth extension… with rotary [movable] parts', main wings with an outer wing 'smoothly jointed' with the fuselage; all-moving horizontal tail-planes and twin all-moving vertical tail-planes (Sukhoi). The central (roughly) section of the fuselage was 'flattened' and formed the basis for a group of aerodynamic elements, the two engines being housed in nacelles, which were widely spaced 'along [a] horizontal line while engine axes are directed at acute angle to plane of aircraft axis of symmetry along flight direction' (Sukhoi). The retractable undercarriage consisted of two single wheel main units and a steerable twin-wheel nose unit (Harkins, 2015).

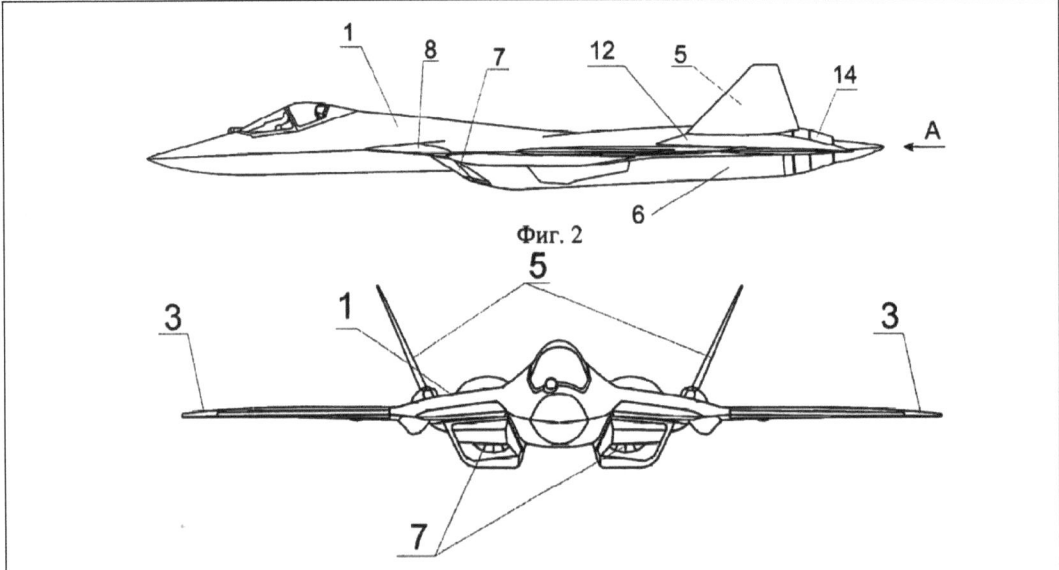

Design characteristics: "… aircraft comprises fuselage **1** with dogtooth extension, with outer wings **3** smoothly jointed with fuselage **1**, all-moving horizontal tail planes **4**, and all-moving vertical tail planes **5** (Designer data). Fuselage middle section is flattened and made up of a set of aerodynamic sections. Engines are mounted in engine nacelles **6** spaced apart along horizontal line while engine axes are directed at acute angle to the plane of aircraft axis of symmetry along direction (Designer data). Said dogtooth extension **2** comprises rotary parts" **8** (Designer data). Effect of design characteristics: 'increased radar deception [low-observability in radio-electronic spectrum], better maneuverability at larger angles of attack and aerodynamic quality at supersonic speeds' (Designer data)

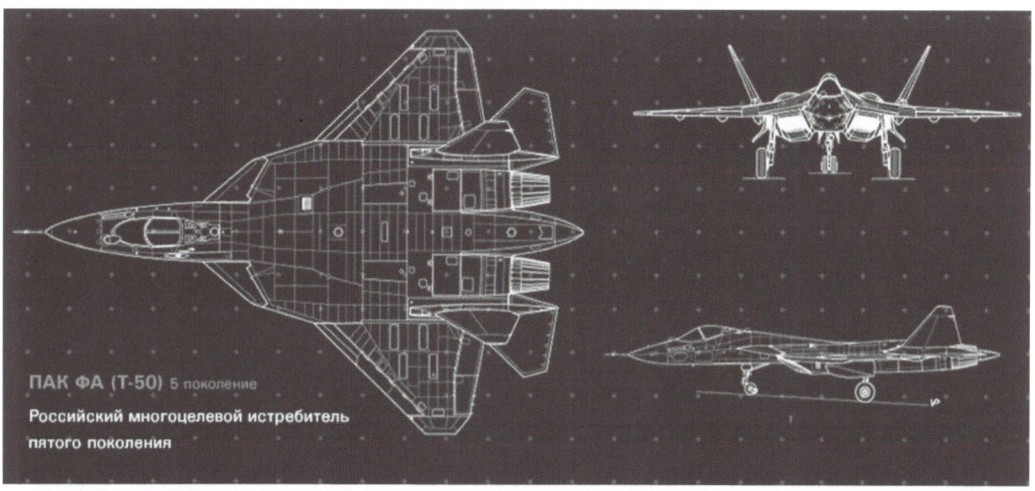

Top: Three-view general arrangement drawing of the T-50 (Su-57) – Control surfaces include TsPVO all moving vertical tail, CSPO all moving horizontal tail, Flaperons to control aircraft roll angles and ailerons. Russian language text basically states that the T-50 was a multipurpose fighter of the fifth generation. Bottom: The eighth T-50 flight development aircraft, T-50-9, during a development test flight. Kret/MODRF

Top: T-50-4 flexes its all-moving horizontal tail planes and twin all-moving vertical tail planes as it taxis at Zhukovsky. Above: The rotary (moving) surfaces of the dogtooth extension are shown in the downward (drooped) position on T-50-5. KnAAPO/Knaaz

Frontal aspect of T-50 development aircraft ground operations illustrating the moving dogtooth extension from fuselage to inner wings in the downward position. UAC/Rostec

Underside view of the forward section of a T-50 flight development aircraft illustrating the rotary extensions located ahead of the engine air intakes. Rostec

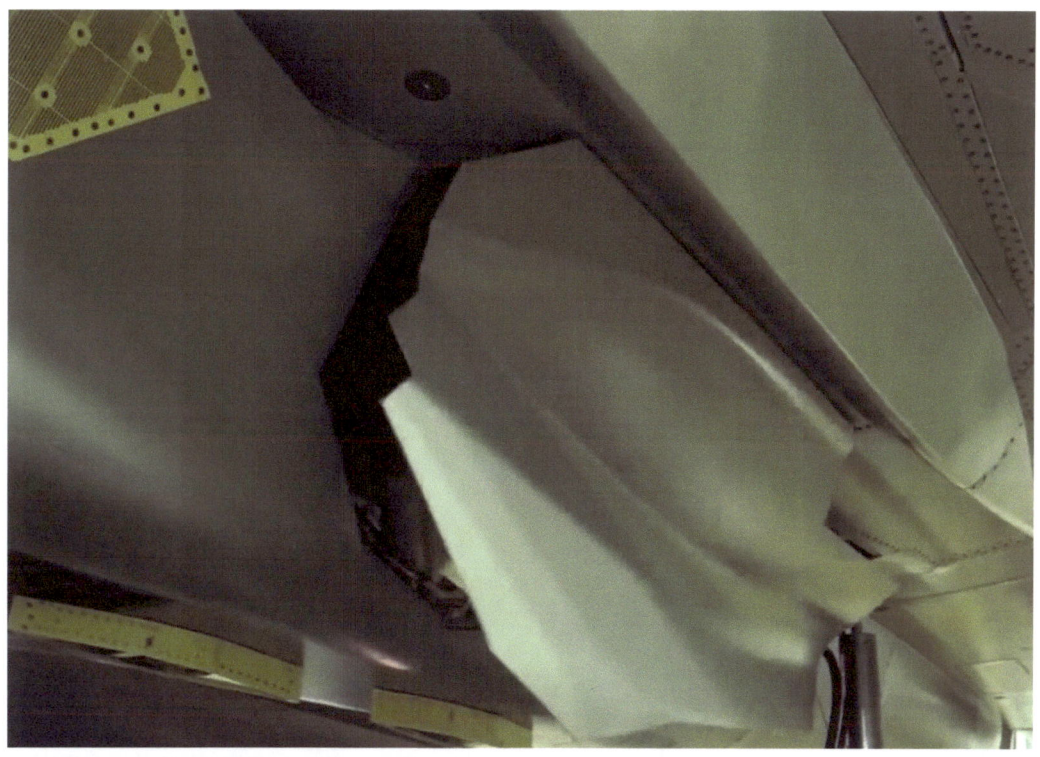

Partially retracted main undercarriage on a serial produced Su-57, illustrating serrated edges to reduce returned radiation, enhancing low-observability. UAC

The fourth T-50 development aircraft, T-50-4. UAC/Sukhoi

Conceived under the auspices of the LFI program the T-50 emerged as a medium size fighter aircraft smaller in overall dimensions and mass than the Su-35S 4++ generation heavy multi-role fighter. Knaaz

The T-50 design featured vastly reduced radar cross section compared with legacy aircraft designs whilst allowing for excellent maneuverability, high angles of attack and enhanced aerodynamic characteristics when flying at supersonic speeds. Overseen by the advanced KSU digital multiple redundant flight control system, the horizontal tails provided the aircraft with control in the longitudinal channel (pitch) during all aircraft flight modes and provided roll control by use of differential mode rejection when at supersonic speeds. The trapezoidal wing planform featured negative sweep on the trailing edge. The design provided enhanced value of chord length at the roots, which corresponded to reduced wing thickness in the area 'at high absolute values of the thickness of the wing', reducing wave resistance in the transonic and supersonic flight regimes (Sukhoi). The leading edge flaps increased the aircraft aerodynamic qualities in subsonic flight regimes, aiding airflow around the wings, particularly when flying at high angles of attack, the flaps also enhancing aircraft maneuverability. Trailing edge flaperons were used to control lift during take-off and landing and aid in providing control of the aircraft in roll in various flight regimes, including supersonic flight. The ailerons aided roll control during take-off and landing. Thrust vector control for the engine nozzles aided aircraft control in the pitch channel at low speeds, providing a driving moment when at 'supercritical angles of attack in conjunction with all-moving horizontal tail surfaces' (Sukhoi). The T-50 design had twin outwardly canted all-moving vertical stabilizers – an assembly of rudders and keels that bestowed stability and control for the aircraft in flight and contributed to aircraft braking by use of differential deviation of the rudders. The design and shaping of the rudders aided in reduction of the aircraft radar signature in the lateral hemisphere (Sukhoi).

The air intakes for feeding the engines were located on the fuselage sides; the inlets being chamfered – cut away – right-angled fringes forming symmetrical sloping edges. The intake design ensured that a continuous flow of air would be fed to the engines during all flight modes, even when the aircraft was flying at extreme high angles of attack, in the region of 100° from the horizontal. The air ducts leading from the intakes to the engines, located in the rear fuselage, were curved to shield the engine compressor from emitting radar signals, thereby reducing the aircraft observability in the radio-electronic spectrum in the forward hemisphere.

It was clear, even at a glance, that low-observable goals were one of the main design drivers for the T-50. This Sukhoi graphic clearly shows such 'stealth' traits as alignment of aircraft surfaces, which, combined with the many other low-observable design features, such as low-observable coatings, bestowed upon the aircraft a typical radar cross section on a par with its western analogues. Sukhoi

Although composites had been used in the manufacture of earlier Russian aircraft designs, with the T-50 the levels of composites in the construction was vastly increased. According to Rostec Corporation, 25% of the aircraft mass and 70% of the surface of the T-50 (Su-57) was constructed of composite materials optimised for the extreme conditions of the aircraft flight regime – subsonic and supersonic. These materials included polymer carbonfibre reinforced plastics manufactured by ORPE Obninsk Technologiya (Obninsk Enterprise Technology), a holding of RT-Chemcomposite. In the areas used, composites reduced mass around fourfold in comparison to traditional manufacture by metal materials in aircraft of the third and fourth generations (TsAGI). As well as reducing weight, the switch to composite materials in aircraft construction resulted in other benefits, including reduced RCS

(Radar Cross Section) – the equivalent surface area of returned radiation energy – through reduction in reflectivity of radio electronic returns, justifying the higher costs (composites are estimated to cost around six times more than the metals previously used for areas, such as wings). The production of composites for the T-50 (Su-57) was accomplished in the same traditional autoclave fashion as that adopted by Boeing and the European Airbus consortium (Harkins, 2015).

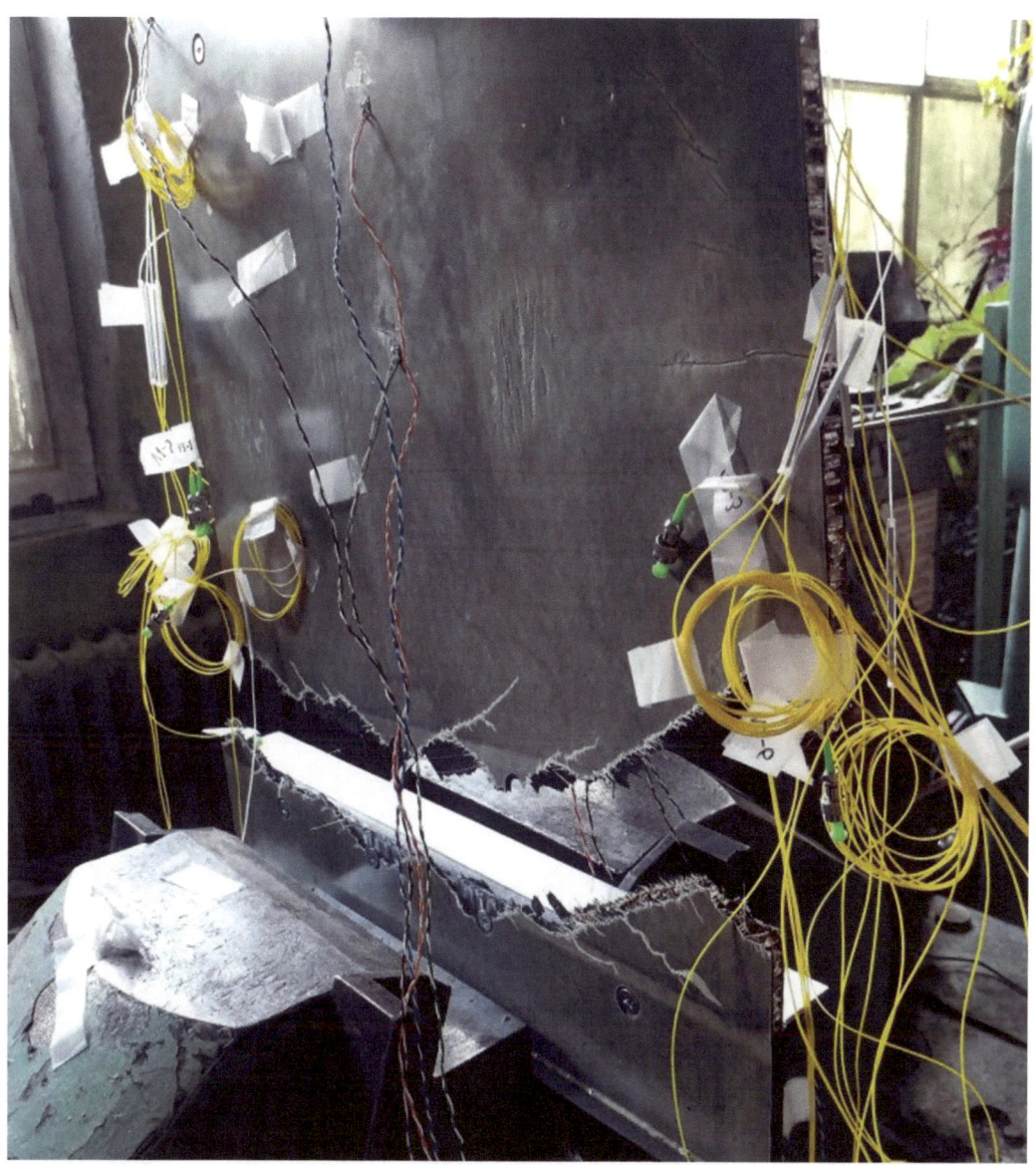

A composite panel is tested to breaking point during T-50 development trials. UAC

Internally the T-50 composite wings, manufactured by Obninsk, was an aluminium honeycomb structure, this being covered, above and below, with around one hundred layers of carbon fiber composites, making up the so called 'Black Wing'

– so named due to its characteristic colour (Rostec). The composite layers were 'cut and stacked using a laser, each at the desired angle. After stacking all the layers together, it is placed in an autoclave for eight hours, during which time it is converted into a light aircraft part' (Rostec). This technique was also used in the production of the Sukhoi Superjet 100 civil airliner (Harkins, 2015).

Impact damage, even microscopic, could be more difficult to detect and manage on composite structures than they would be on metal structures. To aid in such tasks, the Su-57 may, at some date beyond 2021, be fitted with a laser monitoring system to detect impacts, a part of the so called smart skin that would effectively provide an aircraft main computer complex with a structural health update (Sukhoi). A prototype of an Su-57 wing complex, incorporating a series of fibre-optic sensors, was built by summer 2020 and trialed by Sukhoi/SIC IRT (Scientific and Innovation Centre Institute for Research, development and Technology transfer) (UAC).

This T-50 model shows the obvious frontal aspect low-observable traits, such as alignment of surfaces, like the vertical tails being canted at the same angle as the intake walls, and the sloping air feed to the engines. Less apparent frontal aspect low-observable traits included gold coating the cockpit canopy, incorporation of low observable materials, notably in the engine intake walls, and the so called 'smart-skin', which all combined to vastly reduce frontal aspect radar cross section. Rostec

Many areas of the T-50 (Su-57) design were significantly influenced by the multi-spectrum low-observable requirement. The T-50 employed several means to achieve a reduction in surface scattering – aircraft shaping, accommodation of stores in internal bays, application of RAM (Radar Absorbent Material) – for the Su-57, the

Institute of Theoretical and Applied Electrodynamics developed radio absorbing coatings and modern heat-proof enamels were used (Rostec) – the preferred layout for the engines and measures to reduce the thermal and acoustic signatures.

The idea of stealth (attempting to avoid detection by an enemy) had been around for a long time. In regards to aviation it went back as far as World War 1, with the introduction of camouflage schemes. Attempts to detect aircraft in the air through means other than visual also emerged during World War 1, with the introduction of sound location devices that would listen for noise of an aircraft engine to give advanced warning of an impending air raid. Modern stealth technology as it is understood in 2021, such as that applied to aircraft like the American Lockheed Martin F-117A, Northrop Grumman B-2A, Lockheed Martin F-22A, Lockheed Martin F-35 and the Russian Su-57, PAK DA (Perspective Aviation Complex for Long Range Aviation) and Checkmate 5th generation lightweight multifunctional fighter design, could trace its beginnings back to the height of the Cold War in 1960's Soviet Union. The kick-start for the American stealth technology program came about when a paper written by Soviet physicist Peter Ufimtsev (whom apparently worked on the American B-2A bomber program after immigrating to the United States) was published in a Soviet Journal. This *faux pa* by the Soviets allowed the paper to come to the attention of Lockheed, which had been studying ways to reduce aircraft visibility to radio-electronic radiation waves (radar), having already designed the SR-71 Blackbird family of strategic reconnaissance aircraft that had adopted some humble means of reducing radar and thermal signature. However, the large Blackbird still presented a significant radar and an immense thermal signature, being indisputably detected by the Soviet era air defence network (Harkins, 2015).

In short, the meat of Ufimtsev's paper suggested that angular shaping, special paints and construction materials, could make an aircraft very difficult to detect by radar. There were of course drawbacks to such a design that would in effect have to be designed from the bottom up for a specialist role with little to no flexibility. These beginnings led, with much financial commitment and development, to the Have Blue project that spawned the F-117A strike aircraft, which was known by the unofficial label of 'Stealth Fighter'. Although referred to as such, and despite having an 'F' for fighter prefix, the F-117A was a strike aircraft with no air to air capability whatsoever. Its design was far from ideal for an air to air role, this point being clear to Lockheed when it was designing the F-22 air dominance fighter, which was a second generation low-observable design (Harkins, 2015).

In basic terms the operation of a radar reflects radio waves off the surface of an object in its path, revealing its approximate location to the emitting radar, the time it would take for the waves to return to their source being used to determine the approximate range to the radar target. The main goal of so called stealth technology, in regards to aircraft, was to reduce the reflected radio waves, thereby reducing the likelihood of detection, or at least the distance at which the stealth target would be detected. In short, the larger the RCS the easier it would be to detect a target and the lower the RCS the harder it would be to detect a target (Harkins, 2015).

Despite the fact that modern stealth, as it is understood in 2021, was born in the Soviet Union, the Soviets, while being no less attentive to the benefits of stealth technology, were less willing to make sacrifice in other areas of the aircraft combat potential in the adoption of stealth as had been the case with the F-117A, particularly as it was clear that such aircraft could still be detected by modern and certain older generation radar types. That stealth technology was well understood in the Soviet Union was recounted by Victor Chepkin, General Director of Lyul'ka Saturn (now NPO Saturn):

"Together with various institution we carefully analyzed stealth technology and the general principles of invisibility in combat and other contexts. We came to the conclusion, that the hyper-development of stealth – using stealth for stealth's sake – greatly narrowed the range of an aircraft combat potential. Purely stealth aircraft could be used only in a specific set of combat operations and for a particular purpose, and this technology is very expensive" (Chepkin-NPO Saturn).

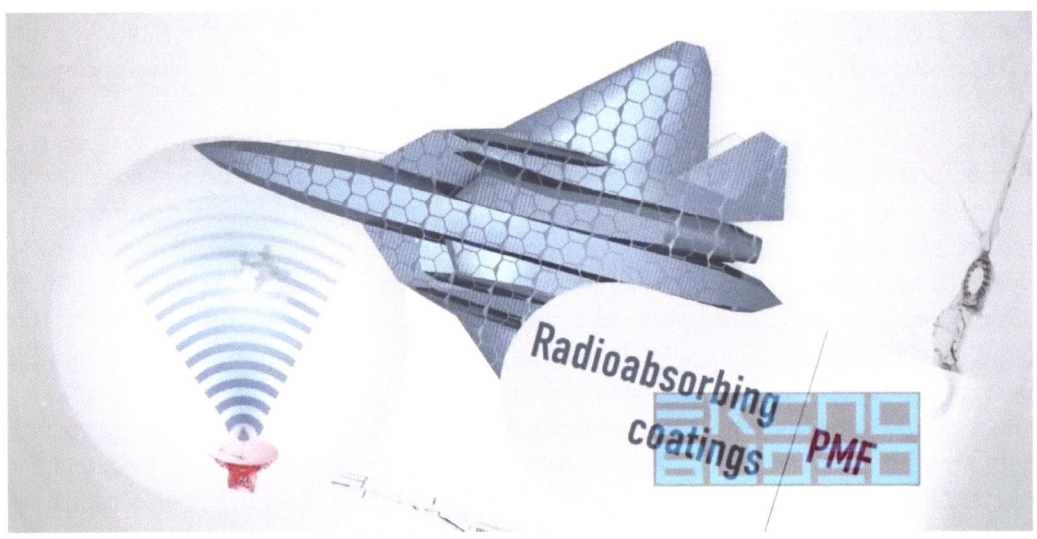

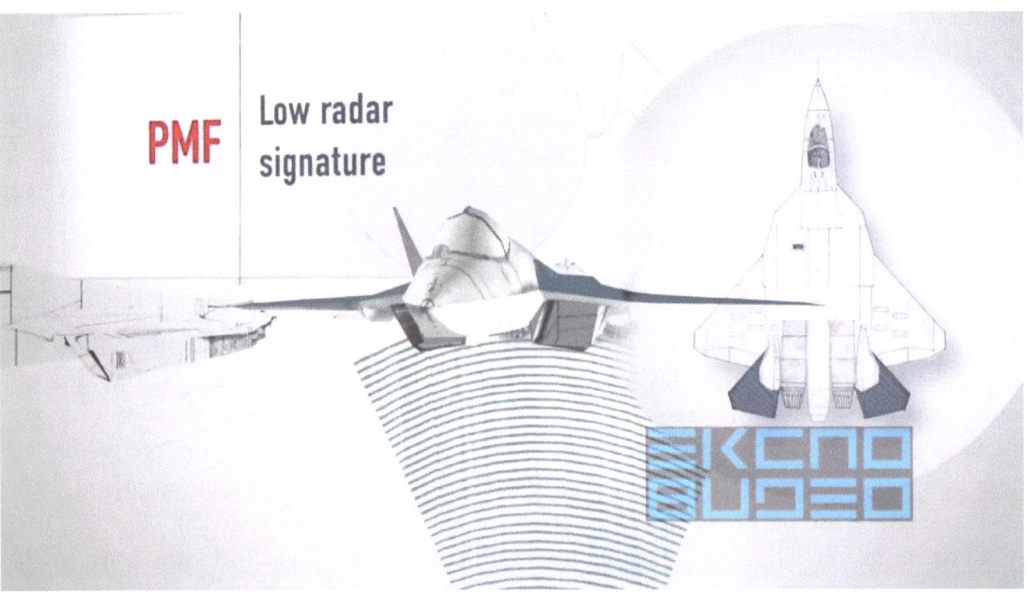

Previous page: Graphics highlighting some of the main areas of the T-50 (Su-57) low-observable characteristics. This page: Alignment of outer line edges contributed significantly to reducing signature in the radio-electronic spectrum. UAC

Although low-observable technology was developed and apparently tested in no less than two different Soviet design bureau (Rostec) under work covering the 1970's and 1980's, its wholesale adoption was decided against by a Soviet commission that concluded that such programs were, on a whole, unaffordable at that time. As the Cold War was reaching its climatic conclusion, eventually culminating with the dissolution of the Soviet Union in December 1991, political resolve and funding remained in short supply. The new Russian Federation that emerged from the ashes of the Soviet behemoth was in financial ruin, leaving scarce funds for military program basics let alone frivolous projects, such as those developing stealth technology. Despite this, many programs ticked along with funding that was drip fed at best. This facilitated for refinement of low-observable technologies to the standard applied to the Su-57, which, despite being a compromise design, the Russians unwilling to relinquish their lead in combat aircraft manoeuvrability, appeared to be on a par with western low-observable designs typified by the F-22A and F-35, certainly in the forward and lateral hemispheres.

The T-50 development aircraft and initial serial produced Su-57 were powered by a pair of AL-41F1 afterburning turbofan engines that allowed the aircraft to supercruise at undisclosed speeds, expected to be below Mach 1.6. This contributed to reducing the aircraft thermal signature at low supersonic speed. Sukhoi

Into the twenty first century, Russia began placing more importance on the application of low-observable technology into new aircraft programs. The 4th++ generation Su-35S and MiG-35/D would incorporate a number of low-observable measures into their respective designs to reduce RCS. However, it was with the T-50 (Su-57) and the PAK DA long-range strategic bomber programs that stealth was allowed, to a very large degree, influence the design of a Russian combat aircraft (Harkins, 2019a & Harkins, 2015).

As the scattering of radar returns off of a target aircraft is in effect what causes said aircraft to de detected by the targeting radar, and the most basic goal of stealth technology was to significantly reduce these returns, the main techniques adopted for the reduction of the T-50 (Su-57) RCS was aerodynamic shaping/external lines to direct radio waves away from the emitting radar and RAM coatings to absorb radio waves rather than reflect them back to their source. The technique for aircraft shaping included designing the outer surfaces 'with an angular shape of straight faces and sharp angles' (Designer data). In this regard, the sweep angle of the wing leading edges (48°), empennage and the air intakes were uniform. This uniformity in sweep angle was carried over to the wing trailing edges (-14°) and tail surfaces. The RAM approach covered certain aircraft outer surfaces with the special coatings and enamels developed by the Institute of Theoretical and Applied Electrodynamics (Rostec) and the engine intake walls were lined with RAM materials.

Another measure taken to reduce radio-wave scattering was to decrease the number of antennas and protrusions on the aircraft exterior. To this end, an integrated antenna feeder system was developed by NPP Polet for the T-50 and the Ka-52 attack helicopter, this contributing to a reduction in radar signature by reducing the required number of antennas on the airframe. In legacy aircraft each sub-system incorporated their own antenna, with up to several tens of antennas on an aircraft, all of which contributed to increasing the aircraft radar signature. The NPP Polet integrated antenna feeder system combined antennas for a range of equipment —communications, navigation, identification transceivers etc. This reduced the number of required antennas. To further reduce radar signature the antennas were built into the fuselage structure, covered by a radar-transparent coating. This practice, as well as reducing the aircraft radar signature, was also less expensive than the previous practice and reduced aircraft drag through reduced wind resistance (NPP Polet).

It could be considered that the main difference between the American approach and the Russian approach to the fifth generation fighter was that the Americans favoured stealth over agility. This can, to a certain degree, be considered the case. However, the Russian approach to producing a more manoeuvrable fifth generation fighter compared to its American analogous has not come at any major degradation in low-observable qualities in comparison to the American aircraft. In regard to low-observable qualities, it is often stated as credence, without supporting data, that the F-22A has a lower radar cross section to that of the T-50 (Su-57). However, this is disputed by Rostec Corporation which emphatically stated that the T-50 had a cross section lower than that of the F-22A, the Americans of course postulating that the F-22 has a lower cross section to that of the T-50. Rostec Corporation stated that the Sukhoi design team 'greatly reduced the effective surface scattering of the PAK FA [T-50]…' with the T-50 returning an 'average value indicator', stated by Rostec as between '0.12 and 1 square meter' (Rostec). By comparison, Rostec claimed the F-22A has a minimum cross section of 0.3-0.4 square meters, these figures apparently coming from T-50 chief designer Alexander Davidenko – the actual F-22A cross section values of course remain classified. Other than the Rostec value for T-50 RCS, a number of values emerged for the RCS of the design. These generally ranged from a high of 0.04 (unverified) to a low of 0.02 m^2 (unverified). Estimates of 0.01 m^2 cannot be qualified and should, therefore, be treated with caution, the 0.12 to 0.02 m^2 value being the most reliable at the time of writing. What is clear is that the RCS of the T-50 (Su-57) is a quantum shift in reduction from the circa 10 m^2 of some fourth generation fighter aircraft and in advance of the range of $4^{th}+$ generation aircraft in service in 2021.

No matter how much an aircraft radar signature is reduced, it would still present a sizeable thermal signature to passive detection systems. However, a number of measures were taken to reduce the Su-57 (T-50) thermal signature, including installation of cooling systems around areas most prone to expelling heat, this most notably affecting the engines, which were also the main areas targeted for reductions in acoustic noise signature. To frustrate visual identification, the Su-57 adopted a digital designed pixel paint scheme to break-up airframe contours (Rostec).

The T-50 is powered by two AL-41F1 afterburning turbofan engines similar to the AL-41F1-S (Article 117S) engines that powered the Su-35S. The 117S (top), which was described as a deep modernised derivative of the AL-31F, was equipped with all-aspect torque variable (thrust vectoring) nozzles (above). NPO Saturn

Engines – The T-50 (Su-57) program is a tale of two engines. The T-50 development aircraft and the initial serial produced Su-57 were powered by two AL-41F1 turbofan engine, from which the AL-41F1-S (Article 117S) engine developed by NPO Saturn Research and Production Association for installation in the Su-35S were derived. Later serial Su-57 for the Russian Aerospace Forces and potential export Su-57E will, under 2021 planning, be powered by two Product 30 (initially referred to as Article 129) Second Stage fifth generation engines. The bypass engines formed the core of the power plant system that included a fire extinguisher, engine management and control systems, auxiliary turbine, auxiliary gearbox and an inlet control system.

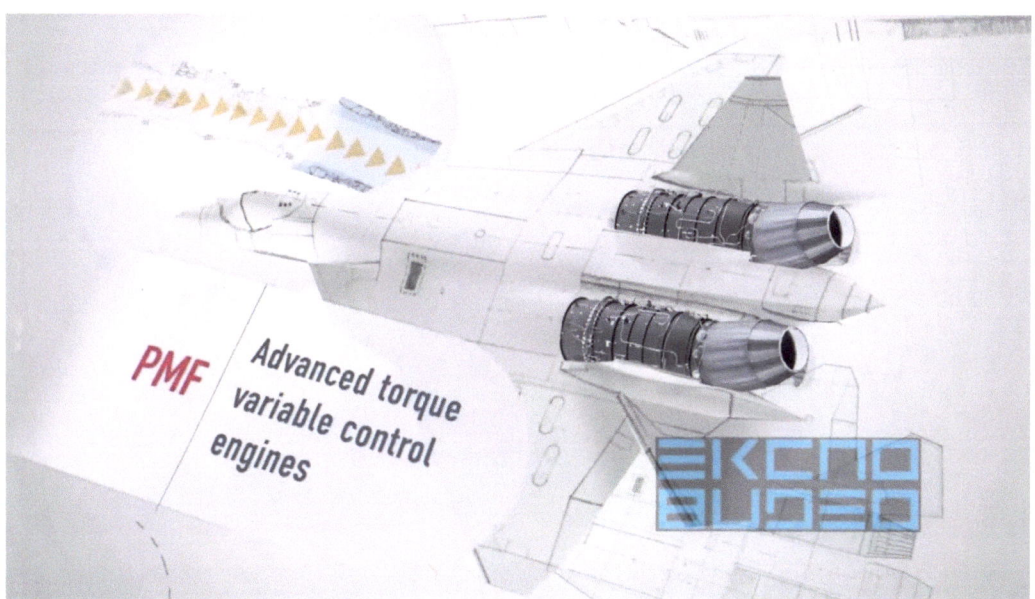

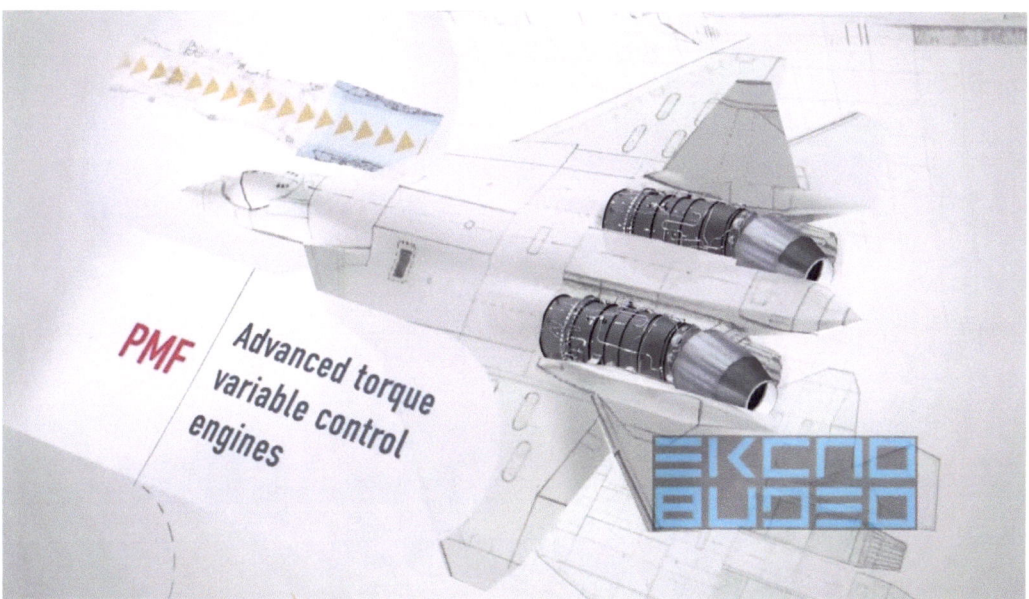

The T-50 engines featured torque variable (thrust vector) nozzle control, which, combined with aerodynamics, control surfaces and the advanced flight control system, bestowed upon the aircraft its excellent super-manoeuvrability and short-field performance, unrivalled by any other fifth generation fighter design. UAC

T-50-8 during development/testing powered by two **AL-41F1** afterburning turbofan engines. UAC

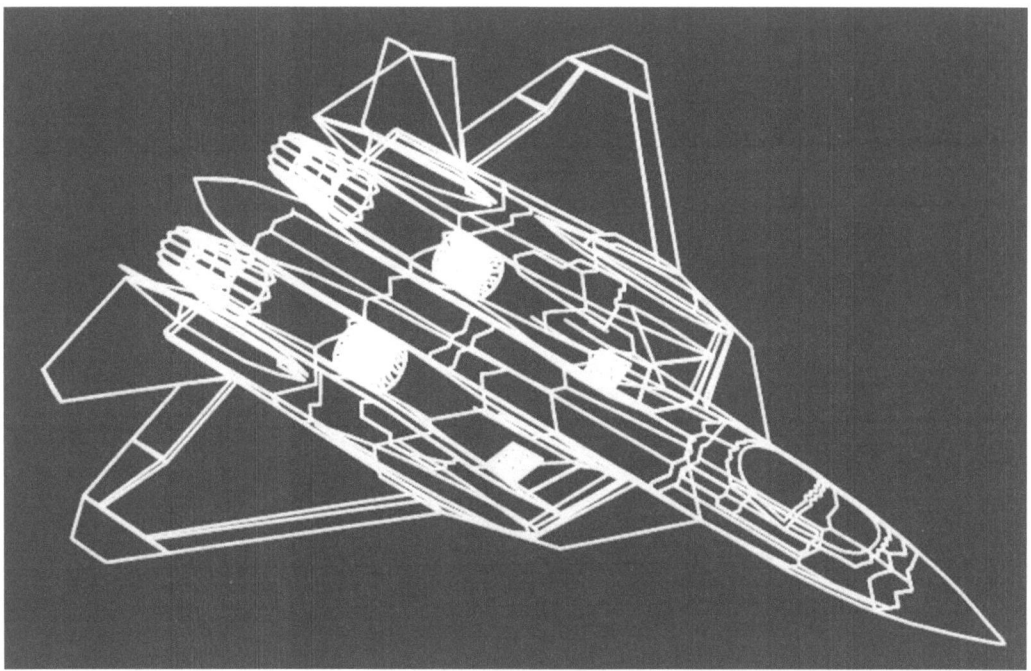

Ghosted diagram of the T-50 (Su-57) detailing the arrangement of the two afterburning turbofan engines in the widely spaced engines bays. UAC

There has been no official release of information for the AL-41F1 engine other than that mass is around 1400 kg and afterburner thrust is in the 15 ton class. Overall ratings were expected to be similar to the AL-41F1-S (117S) variant powering the Su-35S. Production of this engine, which was described as a radically modernised variant of the AL-31F that powered the Su-27 family of combat aircraft, was a cooperative venture between UMPO (Ufa-based Motor Building Association) and Rybinsk based NPO Saturn, both subsidiaries of United Engine Corporation. Although not referred to as such in released NPO Saturn documentation, the 117S was confirmed by United Aircraft Corporation and UMPO as also carrying the designation AL-41F1-S (Harkins, 2015).

The 117S derivative engine incorporated a number of fifth generation features, including a new fan design, new high and low pressure turbine designs, a plasma ignition system, located in the cockpit, and a new digital control system, apparently comparable to the full authority digital engine control system incorporated in western aircraft engines. Available thrust, at 14500 kgf in afterburner mode, was increased by around 16% over that of the standard AL-31F, according to developer data. This, however, would suggest a thrust of just over 12300 kg for the AL-31F as the basis for such a calculation. As the AL-41F1 matured, planned time between overhauls would increase from 500 to 1,000 hours (Harkins, 2015).

Product 30 – The Product 30 Second Stage engine was developed under the PAK FA Prospective Engine Program, about which very little was known in 2021 other than the basic shape and statements from the developers that afterburner thrust would be in the 20 ton class, some 25% greater than the AL-41F1. Released diagrams of the fifth generation engine from designer NPO Saturn showed a different outline to that of the AL-41F1-S of the Su-35S. Information released by NPO Saturn did confirm that the engine for the Su-57 was developed by UEC subsidiary companies, UMPO (Ufa-based Motor Building Association) and NPO Saturn, etc. (UEC).

The nozzle assembly of the AL-41F turbofan engine in the port side bay of a serial produced Su-57 is shown in dry power (top) and in afterburner (bottom) as the aircraft holds for take-off on the post manufacture maiden flight. UAC

A steering committee, headed by Evgeny Marchukov, Chief Designer at A.M. Lyul'ka Experimental of NPO Saturn, was put in place at UEC, UEIA (Ufa (Engine)

Industrial Association), which was designated chief designer for the Prospective Engine Program in 2013. The majority of the authority for management of the engine came under what UEIA referred to as a 'phase-gate system', whereby development was undertaken with clearly defined and identified objectives for respective periods (UEC). The following year UEIA assumed position as the primary manufacturer of prototype engine components and respective assembly tooling, following which the association, in cooperation with Lyul'ka Experimental (NPO Saturn), commenced preparations for demonstrations of the engine (Harkins, 2015).

Data leaks suggested that the Product 30 Second Stage engine had an initial thrust rating of 11000 kgf dry (military power) and 18000 kgf with afterburner (with potential for growth). As was the case with all engines so equipped, the use of afterburner involved burning additional fuel in an afterburner section to temporarily increase thrust, with the drawback of reducing host platform range/endurance, increased thermal signature and increased stress on the aircraft structure/components.

Diagram of the Prospective Engine Product 30 (formerly Article 129). NPO Saturn

The Second Stage engine commenced flight testing when T-50-2 took to the air on 5 December 2017, powered by a single AL-41F1 engine in the starboard engine bay, balanced by a single Product 30 engine housed in the port engine bay. By the end of 2020, several development models of the Second Stage engine had been built for testing. Work was moving toward providing for assembly of serial engines, to be built at the UEC-Ufa Engine Production Association, which was itself incorporated within the structure of Rostec Corporation. One area of benefit for aircraft powered by the more powerful Second Stage engine was enhancement of the ability to sustain supersonic flight without recourse to the use of afterburner.

The Product 30 had been arrived at through a collaborative effort of a number of Russian engine design house/builders. As shown in the accompanying Product 30 diagram, the KDA, KSA section was developed by FSUE Plant (Zavod) and IM V. Ya Klimov – JSC Klimov – (co-primary developers) with FSUE NPP Motor (secondary developer) and manufactured by OJSC UMPO. The TND, Back OPOPS mixer was developed by Aviadvigatel, OJSC (UEC-Aviadvigatel) (primary) and NPP Motor and AMNTK Soyuz, OJSC (secondary) and manufactured by PMZ OJSC. The FK section was developed by NPP Motor (primary) and NPO Saturn (secondary) and manufactured by UMPO. The PRS section was developed by Plant (Zavod) and JSC Klimov (primary) and NPO Saturn (secondary) and manufactured by NPO Saturn. The KND section was developed by NPP Motor (primary), NPO Saturn, Aviadvigatel and AMNTK Soyuz (secondary) and manufactured by UMPO. The gas generator was developed by NPO Saturn (primary), NPO Motor and Aviadvigatel (secondary) and manufactured by NPO Saturn. The PRS section was developed by Plant (Zavod) and JSC Klimov (primary) and NPO Saturn (secondary) and manufactured by Plant Zavod. The SAU section was developed by NPO Saturn (primary) and OAO Star, Plant (Zavod) and JSC Klimov (secondary) and manufactured by OAO Inkar OOO Zem. Visibility in JPS was developed by NPO Saturn (primary), NPP Motor and AMNTK Soyuz (secondary) (NPO Saturn).

The Product 30 turbofan engine was flight tested on T-50-2 (Su-57) flight development aircraft number two when the aircraft alighted with such a unit installed in the port side engine bay, balanced by an AL-41F1 turbofan engine installed in the starboard engine bay. The Product 30 appeared noticeably shorter than the AL-41F1, the engine nozzle of the latter protruding further aft than the former, which adopted serrated features on the rim to aid low-observable qualities. UAC

The AL-41F1 and Product 30 engines included all-aspect torque-variable (thrust vector) control for the nozzles. These units, designed by and manufactured by UMPO, greatly increased aircraft performance, particularly in regard to airborne manoeuvrability, but also in other areas, such as take-off and flight safety. In the nozzle designed for the Product 30, special attention was paid to efforts to reduce radar signature through introduction of an arrangement of serrates on the nozzle rim.

The T-50 (Su-57) adopted the widely spaced engine layout tried and proven on the Su-27 series. This increased survivability by reducing the likelihood of damage to one engine affecting the other and provided space for the internal stores located on the fuselage underside between the engine bays. Sukhoi/UAC

The T-50 design incorporated the widely spaced engine layout typical of the Su-27/30/33/34/35S family, increasing aircraft survivability by reducing the likelihood of foreign object damage to one engine resulting in damage to the other. Other survivability features included explosion protection for the fuel tanks. The widely spaced engine layout also allowed excess space for the two main internal weapons bays to be located on the aircraft underside. Audio-visual documentation released by United Aircraft Corporation suggested side fuselage mounted weapons bays for RVV-MD short-range air to air missiles, but this appears to have been for illustrative purposes and did not correspond to actual stores bays.

No authoritative values have been released concerning internal fuel capacity in the T-50 (Su-57). Although carried on trials, it is unclear if the Su-57 would routinely employ external fuel tanks, such as the PTB-2000 2000 litre capacity unit, to increase range. A retractable in-flight refuelling probe was installed on the port side forward fuselage, just to the fore of the cockpit covering.

Top: underside view of a T-50 development aircraft in flight showing to advantage the under fuselage internal weapon bay area. Bottom: The T-50 and serial Su-57 were equipped with a retractable in-flight refuelling probe, which was installed on the port side forward fuselage, just to the fore of the cockpit covering. UAC

The design of the in-flight refuelling system access doors was conducted with due diligence to the low-observability requirements, particularly in the radio-electronic spectrum. T-50-5 (top) and T-50-1 (bottom) illustrated. KnAAPO/Sukhoi

The Su-57 pilot cockpit was covered by a rearward sliding canopy with a single-piece windscreen to the fore, the upper dash being dominated by the heads-up display complex. Sukhoi

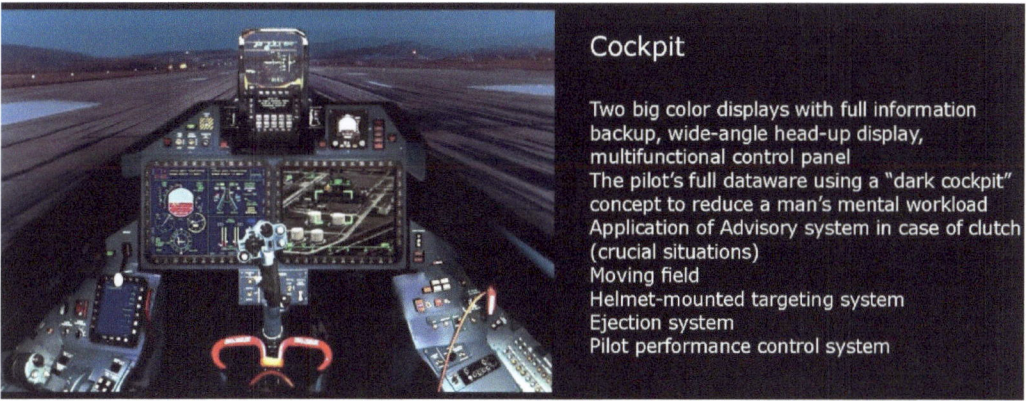

T-50 development aircraft were outfitted with a similar cockpit to the Su-35S (above), there of course being differences in arrangement of displays etc. Sukhoi

The T-50 (Su-57) cockpit canopy and paneling were manufactured by RT-Khimkompozit (glazing was developed by Obninsk Technologiya), and the cabin lights and trim were developed by RT-Chemcomposite. A dominant feature of the T-50 cockpit was a suite of multi-function indicator screen/collimators that provided the pilot with a high level of situational awareness. The initial cockpit layout in the T-50 prototype aircraft was akin to that found on the Su-35S in regard to cockpit displays and HUD (Heads Up Display), with some undisclosed differences. Much of the Su-35S cockpit displays and avionics systems were developed by the Ramenskoe (Ramenskoye) Instrument Design Bureau and companies affiliated with Teknokompleks Research and Production Association. Developer data indicates that the MFI-35 large format colour multifunctional liquid crystal indicator (display) screen, with built in processor, had a resolution of 1500 x 1050 pixels and operated in a *Windows* type system, displaying data sets in various formats – numeric, alphabetic, graphic and symbolic. In addition, the displays could repeat video from the on-board television camera system, which could also superimpose synthesised data in numeric, alphabetic and symbolic formats. The displays were interchangeable, various data being presented on either screen. The integrated IMS (Information Management System), also referred to as the cockpit management system, provided data in both visual and audio formats (Harkins, 2015).

The full-standard serial Su-57 would feature certain enhancements to the cockpit systems, the majority of which, including the multifunctional display screens, were developed by Kret subsidiaries, all incorporated within Rostec (Kret). The multi-function panel with built-in display processor featured a button sub-panel, allowing commands to be conducted easily and rapidly. The function of the airborne collimator, an IKSH-1M, with built-in processor, wide-angle HUD that projected onto the windscreen, was to monitor the environment beyond the cockpit, with an angle of view of 20° x 30° – all necessary flight, stores and other information could also be displayed on the HUD. T-50 development aircraft were equipped with a SHKAI collimator, with wide full-field of view and wide instantaneous field of view, and light emitting diode unit with an integrated computation-graicheskimi means.

The T-50 (Su-57) has been associated with two distinct types of collimator display – HUD (Heads-Up Display). The IKSH-1M, with built-in processor, wide-angle HUD that projected onto the windscreen, would monitor the environment beyond the cockpit, with an angle of view of 20° x 30°. A SHKAI collimator was installed in T-50 development aircraft. Late production standard Su-57 may emerge with a different collimator, although such a requirement has not been publically stated as of 2021. UAC

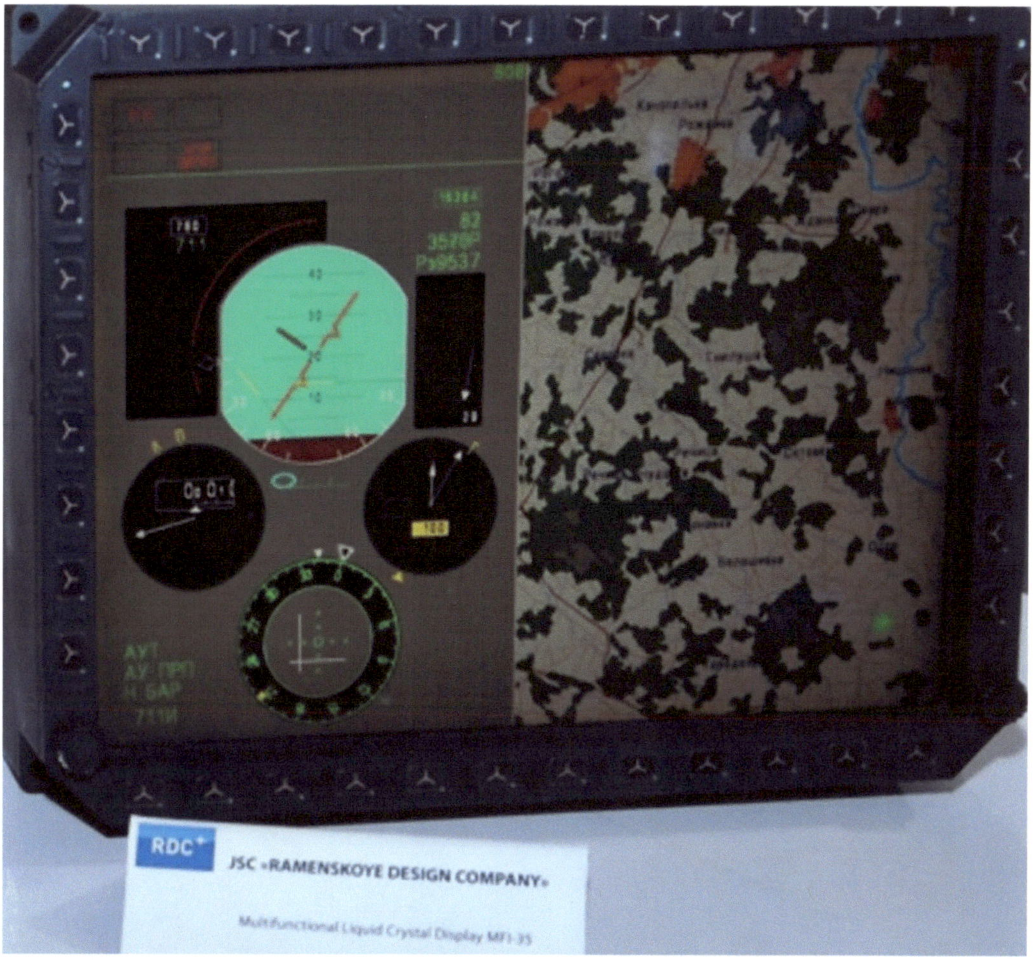

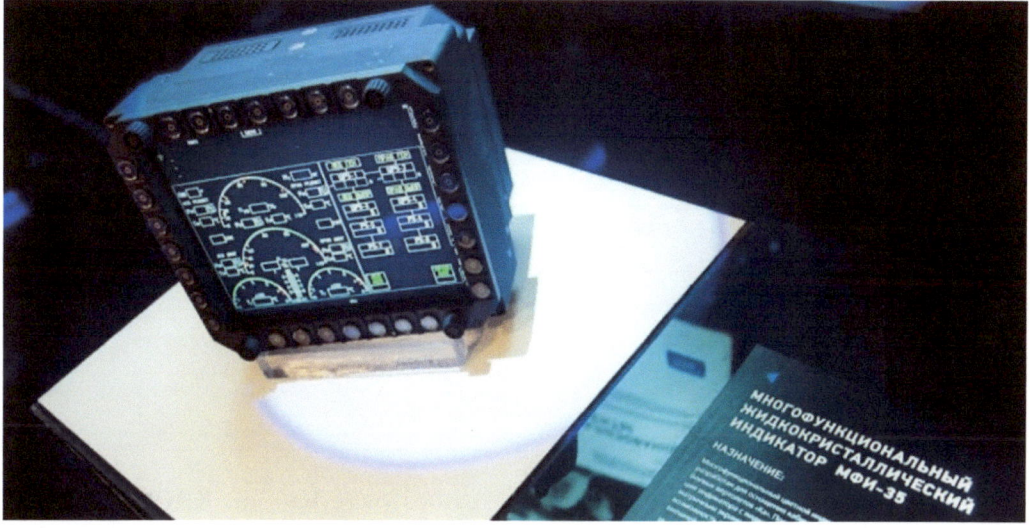

The multifunctional liquid crystal indicator (display screens) that dominate the T-50 (Su-57) cockpit display suite are based on MFI-35 technology. Kret

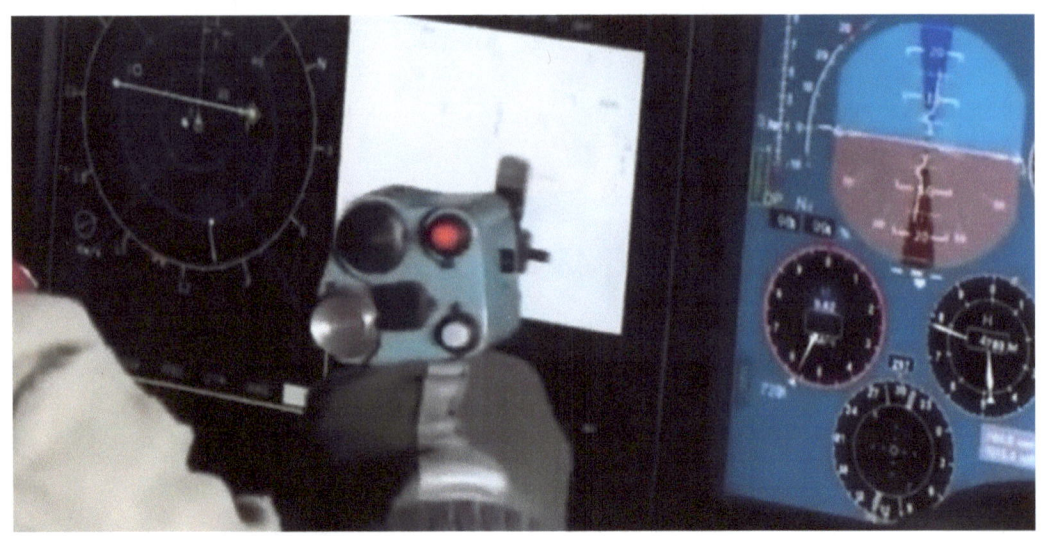

Previous page top: T-50 flight simulator. Previous page bottom: KRUSID Aircraft Throttles Control Stick (HOTAS - Hands On Throttle And Stick) for the T-50. The HOTAS concept allowed pilots to perform many functions at the flick of a switch or press of a button without letting go of the control stick. Aviaavmatika

The cockpit featured KRUSID Aircraft Throttles Control Stick, HOTAS (Hands-On Throttle and Stick) style controls, whereby some aircraft systems and armament could be controlled via buttons and switches located on the pilots control stick.

> **KRUSID Aircraft Throttles Control Stick** (Aviaavmatika data)
>
> Hardware and software of the set consisted of: Reliable compact operating controls based on stacks and eddy current sensors fit for any aircraft type and intended to produce analogue signals of manual control and discrete commands; Operating Controls-to-Avionics Interface Unit (BS OOU); Airplane Control Stick (ACS) and Throttles Control Knobs (TCK).
>
> The ACS and TCK provided: Logic of interaction between crew and avionics; operation in the HOTAS concept and optimal ergonomics of crew workplace and cockpit. The ACS was of minimum size that practically eliminated flight deck shading. Switching components could be implemented as contactless ones.
>
> The OOU interface unit ensured: Operation of standard OOU placed on ACS and TCK, conversion and transfer of data from OOU to avionics via two bipolar serial code lines; Generation of signals to mating equipment as discrete commands of -27V at load current up to 0.2A and -5V at loads current up to 0.015A. The power supply was provided from current generation net of rated voltage 27V.
>
> The operating controls principal of operation covered operating controls of the 'Gashetka-M', '4PS', 'PS3-M' and 'KNM' type, which featured electromechanical contact switches and were designed for generation of discrete commands.
>
> The knob 'KU-S' was based on an eddy-current sensor. When in a magnetic field produced by inductive coils a conducting non-ferromagnetic body was placed, then the body produced a magnetic flow, directed against the coil magnetic flow, that would lead to the change of the coil resistance and current. The change was a wanted signal, and further it was hard and software processed by the BS OOU unit.
>
> 'Gashetka-M' – Contact type electromechanical trigger with tactile effect and forced reset to neutral position. There are three positions: 1. neutral; 2. pre-set; 3. combat mode.
>
> Knob 'KU-S' – Knob KU-S had a floating head automatically backing to neutral position. It generated two analogue signals simultaneously proportional to vertical and horizontal angle of head deflection from its original position.
>
> Tetra-Pole Switch '4P-S' – Tetra-Pole Switch 4P-S was a contact type electromechanical switch with tactile effect. It had a head in an axisymmetric step truncated pyramid. It generated one discrete command in each of its four end positions, and two discrete commands, when pushing the head, which was backing to neutral position automatically.
>
> Three-pole switch PS3-M was a contact type electromechanical switch with tactile effect contact-type, with square arched actuating head (or another form on the user request). It switches discrete commands in each end position and backed to neutral position automatically.
>
> Press button 'KNM' – Press button KNM was an electromechanical button with tactile effect, backing to neutral position automatically and with a function of discrete commands generation.

A virtual reality simulator for the export standard Su-57E was presented at the MAKS-2021 show in July 2021. The simulator incorporated a pair of multi-function display screens (indicators) along with virtual goggles, providing for observing the internal and external environment in high resolution.

Other features of the cockpit included such equipment as the NPP Zvezda K-36D-5 zero-zero ejection seat complex, strain-gauge engine throttles, 'pedals of course control' and an NPP Zvezda ZS-10 helmet, incorporating a HMTS (Helmet Mounted Targeting System) – the cockpit lighting was optimised for NVG (Night Vision Goggle) use. A new HMTS in development for the T-50 was unveiled at the Army-Expo 2015, but the ZS-10 was intended to form the basis of the standard HMTS for initial serial production Su-57 aircraft (Harkins, 2015).

The Zvezda K-36D-5 ejection seat was developed specifically for the T-50 (Su-57) and was incorporated into the design of the Su-35S. The seat was an evolution of the previous generation K-36-3.5 seat installed in Su-30 series aircraft. Developer data showed the improvements over the previous generation seat included:

- extended operating temperature range
- increased range of anthropometry flight crew
- improved performance at the lowest safe altitude ejection with no on-board information about the parameters of flight
- the presence of an electric heated seat and backrest

Ejection could be effected at speeds ranging from 0 km/h up to Mach 2.5 at altitudes from 0-20000 m. The K-36D-5 complex, which weighed no more than 100 kg and included survival equipment, incorporating an RUC-15 oxygen system, was developed by 2013, initial T-50 development aircraft presumably having previous generation or development seats installed during flight testing.

The K-36D-5 zero-zero ejection seat, also installed in the Su-35S, was developed for the T-50 (Su-57) 5th generation fighter. NPP Zvezda

As with all flight helmets, the primary function of the Zvezda ZS-10 remained protection for the pilot from impacts, particularly in the event of ejection. The secondary function was target designation and indication for enhanced engagement of airborne or surface targets, for which a number of advanced sensor/avionics would be incorporated – systems for target designation, data visor (fused into the aircraft sensors/avionics), night vision binoculars, filters to balance light and an KM-36M oxygen mask (NPP Zvezda) – The sighting system for the helmet, which has been referred to under the designation NSTsI-V, was apparently developed by Geofizika-NV. The developer stated that the ergonomics of the ZS-10 helmet, which had been developed by 2011, was significantly in advance of the previous generation helmet of the ZS-7 type.

Previous page: T-50 ejection seat sled testing. This page: The Zvezda ZS-10 helmet replaced the previous generation helmet in serial Su-35S and T-50 (Su-57) aircraft. UAC/NPP Zvezda

For operations at altitudes up to 23.5 km the T-50 (Su-57) was equipped with a KC-50 (KS-50), formerly COP-50, oxygen system, which was smaller than the previous generation KS-129 complex and, through incorporation of a duplicated gas-analysing system, proved to be more reliable than its forebear. Oxygen was supplied to the pilot through a BKDU-50 on-board oxygen installation that produced the oxygen from a reservoir of compressed air fed from the compressor of the gas turbine. The KC-50 system included an RT-17 anti-g valve, which incorporated a mechanism designed to predict anti-g suit inflation.

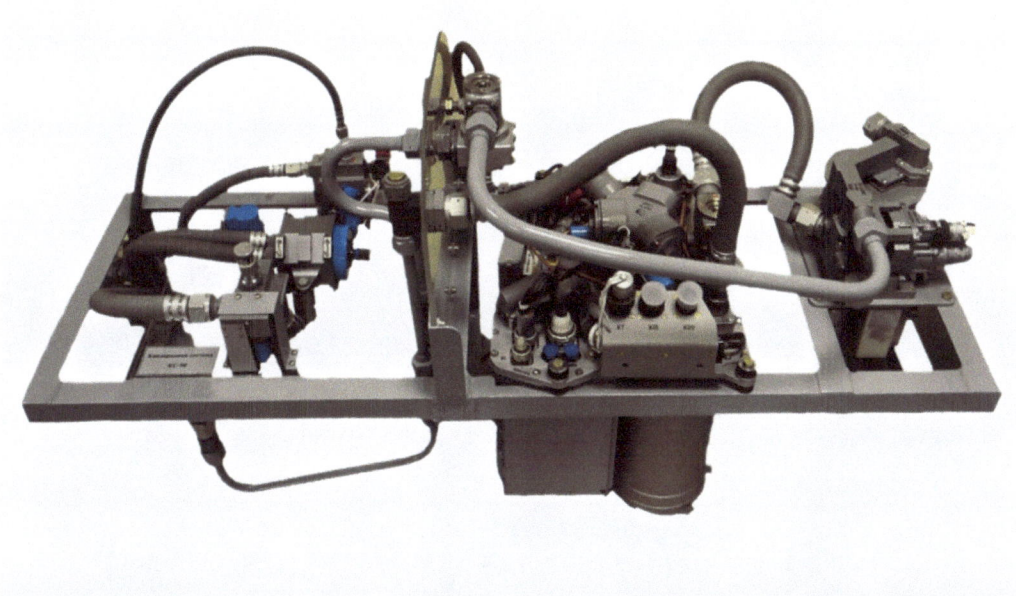

The T-50 (Su-57) was equipped with a KC-50 Oxygen System. NPP Zvezda

The Su-57 pilot would adorn a new generation PKK-7 anti-g (compensating against increased gravity loads) suit, designed to compress the lower body and arms in the event of excessive g-forces being encountered during overload manoeuvres. The suit would be activated through receipt of an electronic signal, emanating from the aircraft information management system, a split second or so before the commencement of the acceleration requiring suit actuation. The basics of the suit, which was provided in several size ranges, were based on heat-resistant fabric with provision for various items of equipment, including cameras. The suit, which weighed around 3 kg, was stated to be several orders of magnitude more efficient than previous generation anti-g suits. If the aircraft encountered a depressurisation then the body chamber and abdominal portion in the suit would expand, resulting in increased compressions in the arms, abdomen and chest regions, along with the additional pressure created in the KM-36M oxygen mask. This allowed the pilot to tolerate excess g forces for longer periods without losing consciousness.

The Su-57 was been cleared for operation at load factors up to 9 g. Excessive overloads of perhaps 9 g lasting a few seconds would not generally be dangerous to a normal fit/healthy body. However, such overload limits lasting for longer periods of perhaps 10+ seconds would place increased strain on the body as the increased gravity overload would render exhaling difficult, making the pilot reliant on the assistance of the anti-*g* suit to avoid losing consciousness, the suit coming into operation within 1 second of the command from the on-board computer.

For operations at altitudes up to the region of 23 km, the Su-57 pilot would be protected by adoption of a VKK-17 altitude compensating suit – weight in region of 3.8 kg – manufactured of dense fabric for insulating and equipped with ventilation to aid cooling.

In order to facilitate the requirement for integration of aircraft sensors, the PAK FA concept that yielded the T-50 development aircraft and the serial Su-57 was equipped with the advanced multiple redundancy IMS noted above. This would oversee management of the aircraft radar and optical sensors, navigation, communications, electronic warfare and other systems that could be coalesced to produce an integrated picture of the overall tactical situation.

The main sensor for the Su-57 was a phased array multi-mode radar system, featuring the main nose mounted active electronically scanned array, operating in X-Band. This unit was one of a whole family of arrays, two smaller units being located on the aircraft sides and a further two on the wing leading edges. Tikhomirov NIIP

Radar and OLS – The Su-57 design incorporated active and passive detection, tracking and engagement systems. The radar complex was a multi-array system that was spread across the aircraft structure under the concept of the 'smart skin' rather than a single unit typically housed in the nose section of legacy tactical fighter aircraft designs. This provided a number of advantages, not least of which was a reduction in aircraft cross section, which consequently did not need to be overly large to accommodate all antenna sections in a single location. The multi-unit approach also provided increased coverage over extended range, increased detection and targeting efficiency and enhanced communications and electronic warfare capabilities.

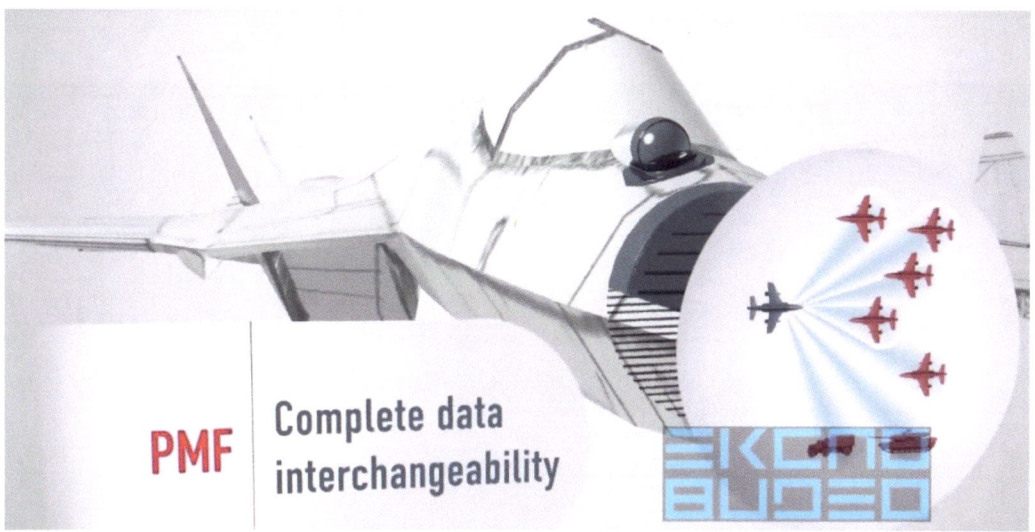

The T-50 (Su-57), which incorporated advanced sensors and avionics with data interchangeability, would become the first completely digital aircraft in the Russian inventory. The graphic depicts an AFAR radar complex from a host T-50 (Su-57) detecting/tracking multiple air and ground targets. UAC

The radar complex, along with the electronic warfare system, has been referred to under the overall designation Sh121 MIRAS (Multifunctional Integrated Radio Electronic System). At the heart of the radio-electronic detection, tracking and targeting capabilities was the AFAR (Active Phased Array Radar), equipped with an AESA (Active Electronically Scanned Array) developed by JSC V. Tikhomirov NIIP Scientific Research Institute of Instrument Design. Statements by George White, CEO of Tikhomirov, referred to the AFAR as being fundamentally different from the traditional conception of what a fighter aircraft radar was. As well as the traditional nose mounted array, the Su-57 featured active radar stations on the fuselage sides and wing leading edges, contributing to the so called 'smart skin'. The radar complex comprised five AESA's, the main X-band system located in the aircraft nose N036 (N036-1-01 – designation unconfirmed), two side fuselage mounted (container) antennas N036B (N036B-1-01 – designation unconfirmed) operating in Ka-band and two L-band antennas (N036L-1-01 – designation unconfirmed) located in the wing leading edges.

The entire N036 radar complex provided vast improvements over legacy systems. Rostec Corporation stated that the AFAR incorporated 1,526 transceiver modules, which extended the range at which targets could be detected and tracked across multiple channels and enhanced the ability to launch missiles against multiple targets (Rostec). The AESA, which utilised GaAs nano-hetrostructures – said nanotechnology remaining shrouded in secrecy in 2021 – and advanced antenna system technologies with electronic beam scanning, arrived at through application of domestic Russian components for the various elements, provided 'for high energy efficiency and a wide range of the beam shapes and operation mode controls (Tikhomirov NIIP). The system incorporated a number of operating modes not found in previous generation Russian aircraft radar.

Extensive bench testing of the active phased array radar was conducted prior to flight testing in the T-50 development aircraft. Tikhomirov NIIP

The AESA angled plane allowed for a sizeable reduction in electron paramagnetic resonance, contributing to an overall reduction in visibility to enemy radar systems, thereby enhancing aircraft low-observable characteristics (Harkins, 2015).

By late 2010, three test X-band AESA's and at least one L-band AESA had been manufactured by Tikhomirov NIIP for testing. Shortcomings in the X-band system, identified during bench testing, were addressed, improvements being incorporated into further development models subsequently manufactured. The AESA was noted to have operated well under various test conditions during climatic and mechanical testing. The difficulties associated with cooling a system so high in power demands was satisfactorily addressed, Tikhomirov apparently employing an 'ingenious' but undisclosed solution to solve the cooling problem (Tikhomirov NIIP).

L-band Active Electronically Scanned Array of the type designed to be fitted into the wing leading-edges of the Su-57. Tikhomirov NIIP

By late 2011, the number of AFAR AESA antenna under test or in manufacture had increased to five, and plans were afoot for the radar complex to be manufactured on a production line at GRPZ (State Ryazan Instrument Plant), which had participated in build of the prototype systems, in particular the distribution system, waveguide runs, transmit-receive module cases etc. (Harkins, 2015).

Tikhomirov tested the advanced transmit-receive modules on the side looking antenna prior to testing them on the front hemisphere AESA, the technologies used in the development of modules for both systems being very similar. Following ground testing, the various components of the radar complex were tested on airborne applications, T-50-3 being equipped with a partial complex assembled from various ground test components before a complete system, apparently the third development radar complex, was flown in T-50-4 (Harkins, 2015).

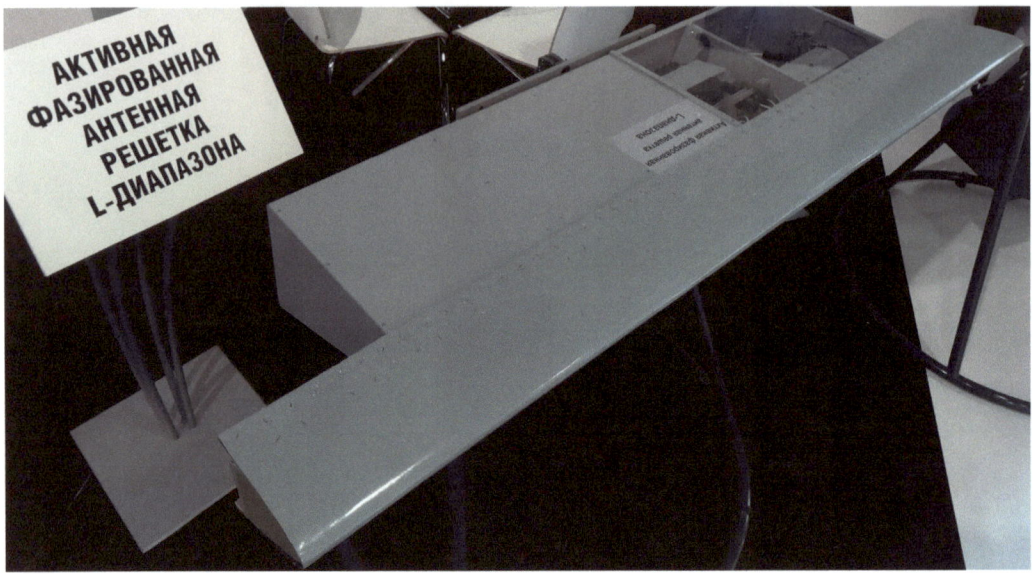

L-band Active Electronically Scanned Array. Tikhomirov NIIP

Tikhomirov NIIP radar systems deputy chief designer, Andrey Sukhanov, stated in August 2015 that the AFAR was 99% ready for serial production. However, when pressed to state how many targets could be simultaneously tracked and the number that could be simultaneously engaged, he would confirm only that it would be 'no fewer than the Su-35S' (Tikhomirov NIIP). In 2021, much of the AFAR program remained under the highest levels of classification. However, a few performance characteristics of the system had been obtained through various means. These suggested a target detection range in the region of 400 km, the ability to track up to 60 targets simultaneously and the ability to target 16 targets simultaneously, the most pressing targets being designated for priority engagement. By contrast, the IRBIS-E installed in the Su-35S had a frontal hemisphere detection range for airborne targets with an absolute radar cross section of 3 m^2 of 340-400 km. The number of targets that could be simultaneously tracked and the number that could be simultaneously engaged were put at 30 and 8 respectively. In regard to detection range, this, as stated by Tikhomirov Director General, Yuri Belly, was in excess of that available for any other in service fighter aircraft design. AFAR target recognition and classification capability was also enhanced over that available for the IRBIS-E, as was resistance to ECM (Electronic Counter Measures).

The streamlined nose section was spacious enough to accommodate the X-band AFAR and the OLS, offset to starboard just ahead of the cockpit windscreen. UAC

The AFAR system was endowed with an air to surface capability in advance of that available for the IRBIS-E, which boasted a synthetic aperture radar mode with a resolution of under 1 meter, real beam mapping mode, Doppler beam sharpening mode, ground moving target selection, terrain following flight and tracking of up to four ground targets. Four ground targets could be selected and tracked simultaneously in a number of map generating modes with a variety of resolutions out to a range of 400 km, whilst maintaining active monitoring of the airspace (Harkins, 2015).

The AFAR radar system was complemented by the Optical Location Station, the main elements of which were located ahead of the windscreen, offset to starboard. KnAAPO

The use of radar in the Su-57, as in all aircraft so equipped, increased proportionately the chance that said aircraft would be detected and subjected to countermeasures or direct attack. The Su-57 featured a passive detection, tracking and engagement capability in the form of an OLS (Optical Location Station (System)) developed by UOMZ (Urals Optical & Mechanical Plant). This systems capabilities, much of which remain classified in 2021, were assumed to be in advance of those of the OLS-35 developed by the JSC Scientific and Production Corporation for the Su-35S. The Optical Location Station has been referred to under the designation 101KS Atoll, broken down to 101KS-V(N) for the infrared search and track system located ahead of the windscreen and 101KS-O for the laser countermeasures located on the aircraft uppers surface aft of the cockpit canopy – this latter complex is tasked with targeting infrared guidance systems of incoming missiles to degrade their ability to home on the host aircraft.

The OLS could detect and track targets passively through their emission of thermal radiation (heat), reducing the likelihood that the host aircraft would be detected and subjected to countermeasures. The OLS-35 system installed in the Su-35S had a stated range against a non-afterburning airborne target of up to 50 km with the target in the rear on aspect, and 90 km with the target in the head-on aspect, with simultaneous tracking of several targets – four airborne targets could be simultaneously tracked (Sukhoi). Other features of the OLS included laser ranging and target laser illumination for laser guided ordnance, the OLS-35 system being capable of air to ground ranging out to 30 km and air to air ranging out to 20 km (Harkins, 2015). It would be logical to assume that the parameters of the Su-57 OLS would surpass those of the OLS-35.

The T-50 (Su-57) avionics/antennas were distributed across the aircraft structure, including an avionics bay located aft of the cockpit section. NPO Saturn

Communications, Navigation and Electronic Warfare Systems – In 2004, work commenced at JSC NPP Polet Scientific and Production Enterprise (formerly Gorky Radio Research Institute) on development of an advanced communications system for incorporation into Russia's planned fifth generation combat aircraft. The research and development effort yielded the S-111 (C-111) communications complex, which was installed for the maiden flight of the T-50-1 prototype (NPP Polet). The S-111 communications suite installed on the T-50 development aircraft and serial Su-57 was more advanced than the S-108 installed on the Su-35S. This latter system, which allowed data exchange in automated mode, included two encrypted UHF/VHF radios, a Link-16 equivalent encrypted data-link exchange terminal, a facility for automated exchange of data across radio-links and an encryption system for voice and data communication transfers. In the S-111, large volumes of data, including voice communications, video/surveillance cameras and transponders could be transmitted over centimetric-band radar at speeds up to 34.3

Megabits/second to recipients, including other aircraft in the formation. The system, which featured a digital open architecture, included a reprogrammable platform capable of storing and recording a number of operating procedures – functions performed by separate systems in previous generation aircraft. The modular approach to the system allowed the number of operating channels and functions to be increased. Installed on prototype T-50 aircraft, testing of the system was completed circa 2015/2016, paving the way for serial production at NPP Polet (NPP Polet).

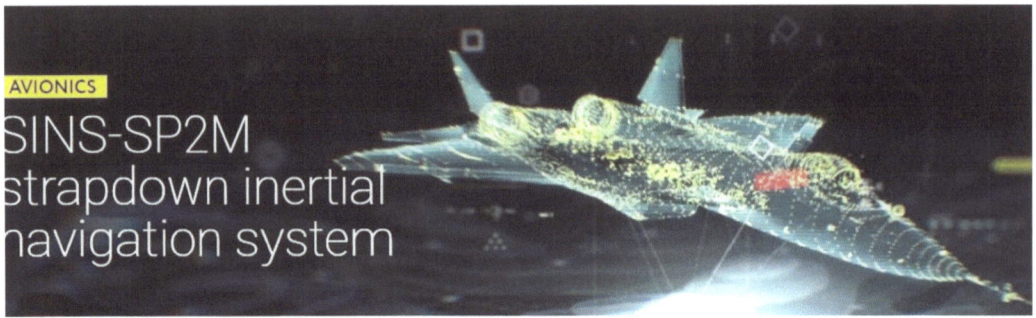

The T-50 (Su-57) was equipped with a BINS-SP2M (also referred to as SINS-SP2M) strap-down inertial/satellite navigation system/radio navigation system, the major elements of which were located in the avionics bay aft of the cockpit section. Kret

The T-50 (Su-57) was equipped with an enhanced variant of the BINS-SP2M strap-down inertial/satellite navigation system/radio navigation system installed on the Sukhoi Su-35S 4th++ generation fighter. This system, developed by MIEA (Moscow Institute of Electro-mechanics and Automatics) and Ramensky Instrument Engineering Plant, subsidiaries of Kret, processed various flight and navigation data autonomously, providing position and parameters of motion without the presence of a satellite navigation function. The system could also utilise data supplied by the GLONASS (Globanaya Navigozionnaya Sputnikovaya Sistema - Global Navigation Satellite System), the Russian Federations orbital cluster of navigation satellites. The whole system was centred around laser gyros and quartz accelerometers – a suite of instruments that provided the ability to accurately determine the velocity of objects in motion. The Su-57 capability for network-centric operations was considerably enhanced through the BINS-SP2M with GLONASS, as such operations required respective forces, be they air, land or naval, to be fused into a centralised network (Kret).

The T-50 (Su-57) was designed to incorporate a significant self-defence capability arrived at through a number of measures, low-observability and active and passive countermeasures systems to the humble infrared decoy. This included a LDIRCM (Laser Directed Infrared Counter Measures) complex (noted above), similar in function to the JSC NII Ekran LDIRCM complex installed on a number of airborne platforms – this system was designed to interfere with the guidance system of missiles directed at the host platform or other aircraft in the group (noted above).

Laser Directed Infrared Counter Measures complex. Kret

JSC KNIRTI KRRTI (Kaluga Research Radio Engineering Institute), a subsidiary of Kret, was tasked with development of a new generation aircraft defence system. This included an advanced electronic warfare jamming complex for incorporation into the T-50 (KRRTI). This emerged as the RZB Himalaya EW complex designed to enhance protection of the host platform through increased electronic jamming/interference immunity.

The Laser Directed Infrared Counter Measures complex was located on the Su-57 upper fuselage just aft of the cockpit section. MODRF

In October 2014, Rostec Corporation announced that KNIRTI (development) and Stavropol Radio plant Signal (manufacture), had delivered the first batch of the Himalaya EW system developed for the T-50. The Himalaya suite, which included transceivers, optical rangefinders, active and passive radar that were completely integrated into the aircraft structure under the 'smart skin' concept, was designed to protect the aircraft/systems against jamming and could generate active and passive impediments to the operation of missile seeker heads launched against the host platform. The system could also counter, 'to a great extent, the effects of low-observability (stealth) technology of enemy aircraft' (Rostec). This was touched upon by the KNIRTI Director General whom added that the Himalaya system 'not only increases noise immunity and combat survivability… but also to a large extent neutralizes the technology to reduce visibility of the enemy' (KNIRTI).

Other equipment developed for the T-50 (Su-57) included the BKS-50 analogue to digital converter, SIMS-50 low-speed measuring system and the SSS-50 warning light system (Kret). Other features of the T-50 (Su-57), outlined by Rostec Corporation, included automatic target recognition, transmit-receive modules that were built into the aircraft skin, reacting to the aircraft surroundings to send warning signals if a threat was detected. Rostec also stated that the T-50 was equipped with the Ryazan developed on-board phased-array radar station, also found in other aircraft, including the Su-35S, some Su-30 variants and Mi-28 and Ka-52 helicopters. A new power supply system, twice as powerful as the previous Russian system, was also developed for the T-50.

The Su-57 may at some point in in the future be equipped with a towed decoy system, such as the Active Towed Radar Trap developed by Scientific Research Institute Ekran. This system, which operated in the 60-70 decibel range, provided protection for the host aircraft from radar homing missiles targeting the aircraft in front and rear semi-spherical 'granules, grades' with azimuth of ±60° and elevation angle of ±22.5° (Kret).

Graphic detailing basic technical/performance characteristics of the T-50 PAK FA (Su-57) – crew, 1; flight duration, 5.8 hours; combat load, 10000 kg; speed, 2600 km/h; range of flight, 5500 km and lifting speed (climb rate), 330 m/s.

Russian language with English translation in parenthesis and italics: особенности авиационного комплекса *(features of the aviation complex)*: Сверхманевренность *(super manouverability)*; Малозаметность *(invisibility [low-observability])*; Сверхзвуковая крейсерская скопость без использования форсажа *(supersonic cruising without using afterburner)* and Короткие взлет и посадка *(short take-off and landing [capability])*

The right hand section of the graphic depicts the various components of the radio-electronic and EW equipment on the T-50 airframe: Комплекс РЗБ гималаи, Разработчик Калужский начыно-исследовательский радиотехнический институт Увеличение помехозащенности и боевой живучести самолета *(The developer Kaluga Scientific Research radio-technical institute increase interference immunity and combat survivability [of the] aircraft)*

Комплекс рлс Крыльевые рлс s АФАР л-диапазона Контейнерная рлс s АФАР Ка-диапазона *(Radar complex, wing radar s AFAR [operating in the L-band] and container radar with AFAR operating in the Ka-band)*, Бортовые рлс с АФАР х-диапазона

(Airborne radars with AFAR [operating in] x-band

Датчики рлс с АФАР, распределенные по обшивке - умная обшивка *(radar sensors with AFAR distributed across the skin – smart skin)*

Система дозаправки в полете *(system refueling in-flight)*

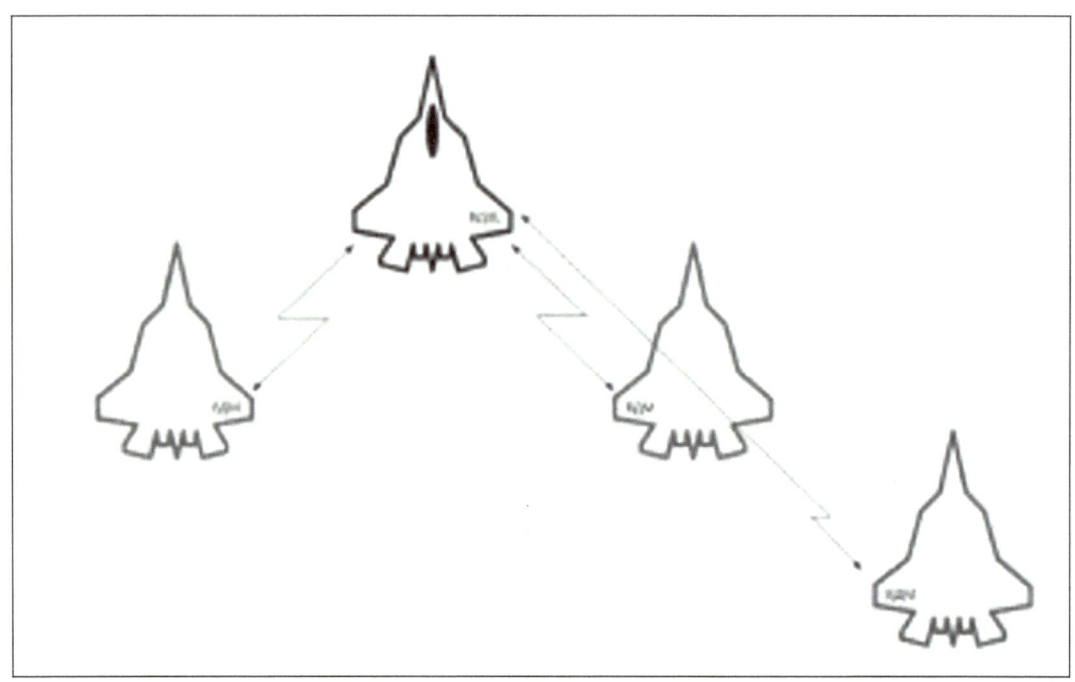

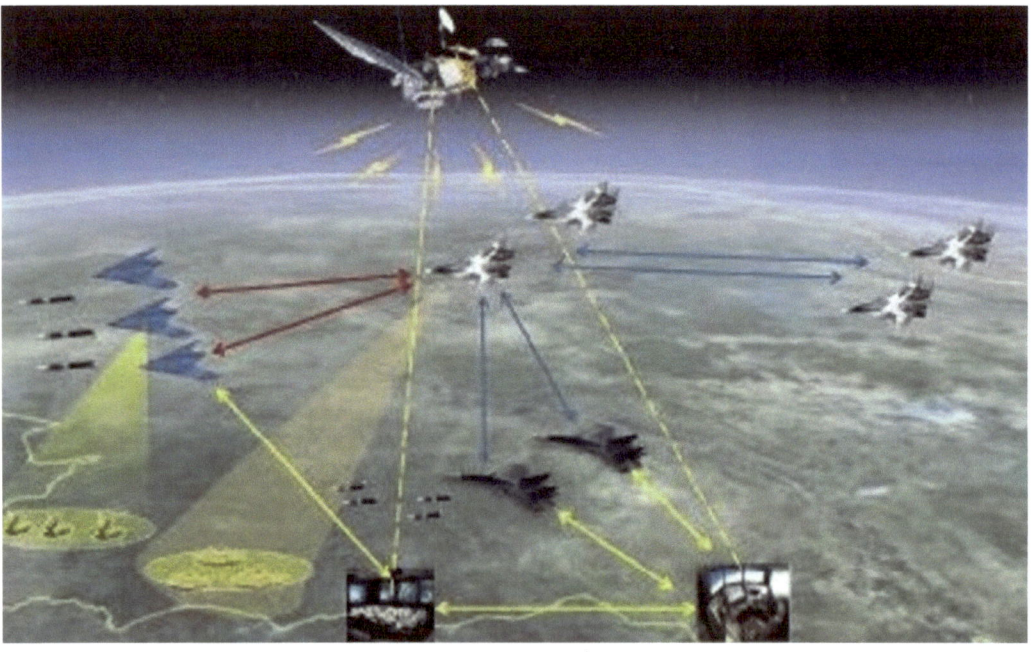

Two graphics depicting a group formation of Su-57 with the lead aircraft controlling three other aircraft (top) and the operation of a group of four Su-57 interacting with multiple off-board systems, ranging from Su-30SM multifunctional strike fighter aircraft, uninhabited aircraft and ground control centres. Sukhoi

The integrated architecture for the onboard networked systems – within the realm of the centralised information management system – incorporated within the Su-57, built on work conducted in studies from the late 1990's/early 2000's, work conducted on the Sukhoi Su-35S, and would be further refined to feed into other programs, including the S-70 Okhotnik uninhabited strike/fighter and the Checkmate 5th generation lightweight fighter. Such work enhanced the multi-functionality and multi-platform integration of Russian fifth generation aircraft.

The Su-57 *modus operandi* involved the use of sensor fusion to enhance operations against a wide-spectrum of airborne, ground and sea surface targets at ultra-long range down to close range. MODRF

The avionics/sensor suite provided for real-time transfer of data between the Su-57, other aircraft operating within the tactical air group, external airborne assets and surface control stations. The Su-57 featured enhanced sensor fusion, a high degree of automated control of systems and a complex of intelligent crew support, all of which enhanced functionality and reduced piloting workload. This allowed for pilot concentration on other mission areas, such as targeting, rather than on flying the aircraft (UAC/Sukhoi). Intellectual support for the Su-57 pilot was present in the ability for the integrated systems/data management system to present a picture and forward recommendations to the pilot on a course of action, such as what weapon(s) should be employed for a given task etc. In addition, the intellectual support provided automatic control modes for the Su-57 onboard systems, including the integrated flight systems, employment of the advanced computer system – referred to as the electronic co-pilot – enabling the occupant to refrain from piloting tasks (noted above). By 2021, the Su-57 cockpit had been developed to the stage of 'maximum automation of the routine processes of piloting and operational use' (Rostec, 2021). This level of automation was confirmed by the head at the Cockpit Department of Sukhoi Design Bureau. Sometime prior to this, a point had been reached whereby the pilot, following take-off, would not necessarily be required to fly the aircraft, instead focusing on other mission areas (noted above), and would not necessarily be required for piloting input again until the aircraft was on the approach for landing – it should be noted that the take-off and landing processes for the Su-57 also incorporated a high level of automation. A function, which enhanced aircraft safety, was that, if for whatever reason the 'pilot stick is released upon take-off the aircraft will manoeuvre itself into a horizontal position. If the pilot is incapacitated then the aircraft will automatically return the aircraft to a pre-designated base and land' (Sukhoi).

Two Su-57, one in lead and one in trail, climb out above the runway during a development test flight. MODRF

The advancements made with development of the Su-57 led to a transformational shift in capability over that of the Su-35S $4^{th}++$ generation strike fighter aircraft, becoming the first completely digital combat aircraft to enter service with the Russian Federation Aerospace Forces. Even prior to serial produced aircraft being delivered, the Su-57 was being referred to as a transitional design leading to a new sixth generation fighter aircraft, studies of which had been underway in Russia from the second half of the 2010's. Technology advances would also feed into the Checkmate 5th generation lightweight fighter unveiled by Rostec/UAC in 2021.

Whilst the past principles of faster, higher, farther had reached a plateau in the 1960/1970's, in regard to tactical strike fighter aircraft, such traits as high-speed, high operational ceiling and long-range/endurance had not lost any importance in the age of advanced avionics/sensors. Rather, their significance remained, but was added to by the enhancement of capabilities through advancements of technology available for avionics/sensors, integration with other platforms through networking with other assets in the aviation group and surface stations etc. and incorporation of early artificial intelligence aids to enhance automation in all aspects of flight. The Su-57 appeared to have achieved an excellent balance between airframe performance and system performance, certainly the former being in advance of that achieved by fifth generation fighter designs emanating from western nations. In regard to onboard systems and weapons, the Su-57, F-22 and F-35 all possessed advantages and disadvantages over each other, the Su-57 and F-22 having clear advantages in an air superiority fighter role over the F-35.

Direct comparisons of the Su-57 and its western counterparts is fraught with difficulties, the Russian aircraft having obvious advantages as a pure air performer, whilst all fifth generation fighter aircraft designs would possess areas of advantage and disadvantage over their counterparts, even without considering force enhancers such as AWACS (Airborne Warning and Control System). Even the theatre of operations would have a significant impact on the outcome of peer capability air to air engagements as this would determine what side had the better access to off-board systems coverage, such as AWACS and ground based radar systems.

Page 87: T-50 (Su-57) at MAKS-2019 (top) and casting a shadow on a runway (bottom). This page: The T-50 design (T-50-1 top) was a more streamlined (sleeker) design compared with the F-22 Raptor (bottom), the American aircraft having a deeper fuselage and clearly larger, in height and area, vertical tails. KnAAPO/USAF

At 2021 planning the Su-57 may possess the better air superiority armament suite in the shape of the RVV-MD, RVV-SD and RVV-BD air to air missiles, the latter having an engagement range considerably in excess of the AIM-120C/D variants arming the F-22. Non-passive, the Su-57 AFAR and F-22A's APG-77, like all combat aircraft radar systems, could be and would be detected by an adversary in a modern $4^{th}+$, $4^{th}++$ or fifth generation fighter aircraft, although at what range(s) remains something of an enigma. The Su-57 would also bring to the fight the advantage of a passive optical location system, which was currently (2020) lacking on the F-22 (an electro-optical system was expected under F-22 update plans). Against a Su-57 in the frontal hemisphere an F-22 would, in all probability, be detected by the optical location station through the formers heat signature, which, although vastly reduced over that of fourth generation aircraft, was still a considerable heat source, particularly as the F-22 accelerated to gain launch energy for its air to air missiles release (Harkins, 2015).

The T-50 (Su-57) was designed with reduced reflective surface area as a design driver, but not to the point of adversely affecting aerodynamic and maneuvering performance. UAC

As this is written in 2021, most performance parameters for the Su-57 remain classified, requests for such by the author, as expected, being politely declined as they had been in 2015. However, as was the case for the 2015 volume, occasionally information would surface in interviews, either inadvertently or deliberately leaked, and some values could be inferred from available technical data on aircraft systems. For example: the T-50 (Su-57) aircraft was equipped with a KC-50 oxygen system specifically designed for operations up to 23.5 km altitude. It could, therefore, be inferred that Su-57 could operate at such altitudes, although normal operating ceiling was expected to be somewhat lower.

In 2015, Rostec Corporation put the T-50 maximum speed at 2500 km/h. The same entity also stated that the aircraft was 500 km/h faster than the F-22, which apparently had a speed in the Mach 2 (around 2400 km/h) range. It is possible, if not probable that the Rostec value of 500 km/h faster was in regard to the F-35 which, at Mach 1.6 maximum speed, fell way down the performance table in comparison to the T-50 (Su-57) and F-22. Complicating matters further, in 2016, Kret, a Rostec subsidiary, released a document stating maximum speed for the T-50 as 2600 km/h. Confusion remained abound in 2021 when Rostec released a new document stating Su-57 maximum speed stood at 3000 km/h (Rostec). This latter value may be erroneous or may refer to potential speed for the Su-57 updated with the Product 30 Stage Two engine, which has thrust values considerably in excess of those of the AL-41F1 powering the T-50 development aircraft and early serial produced Su-57 delivered to the Russian Aerospace Forces from December 2020.

In 2016, Kret released a value for range, 5500 km, with an endurance of 5.8 hours, reinforcing previous claims by the developers that the T-50 (Su-57) would be endowed with longer range on internal fuel than any other fifth generation fighter in service or development. It is clear that the Su-57 built on Sukhoi's experience of producing fighter aircraft with exceptional operational range in comparison to their analogues. Range could be increased via the use of in-flight refuelling, a retractable in-flight refuelling probe being located on the port side forward fuselage just ahead of and below the cockpit (noted above).

Page 90-91: The Su-57 was designed for operations at upper (circa 23 km) and ultra-low altitudes. MODRF

The 2016 document released by Kret put climb rate at 330 metres/second (19800 metres/minute) (Kret), considerably ahead of western analogous and the Su-57 stablemate, the Su-35S, the latter standing at 280 metres/second at 1000 m altitude (Sukhoi). Being considerably lighter than the Su-35S, the T-50, assuming similar engine thrust, would be expected to have a greater acceleration than the Su-35S, which, at an altitude of 1000 m with 50% internal fuel, could accelerate from 600 km/h to 1100 km/h in 13.8 seconds, and accelerate from 1100 km/h to 1300 km/h in 8.0 seconds (Sukhoi).

The USAF publicly states that the F-22 can out-manoeuvre all in-service and projected fighter aircraft and has higher speed and 'greatly extended range' over same. Hard facts reduce this to propagandistic statements that cannot be qualified in the face of performance values coming out of the Russian 4++ and fifth generation fighter programs. In regard to the Su-35S 4++ and Su-57 5th generation fighters, both have proven to be more manoeuvrable, possess higher speed and operating ceiling and greatly outrange the F-22. F-22 ferry range is stated as 2977 km, speed is Mach 2 class, ceiling, 15 km. F-22 engines are rated at 15875 kg, only slightly above the 14000+ kg of the Product 30, whereas the F-22 has an operating weight of around 38000 kg against the Su-57 circa 22-24000 kg. On these values the Su-57 possesses a higher thrust to weight ratio of excess power over the F-22. Perhaps an acknowledgment of the physical shortcomings in the F-22 design over those of the Su-57, it was reported in May 2021 that the USAF commander was mooting early retirement of the former. However, with any American sixth generation fighter some considerable number of years off, the F-22 will likely remain the main air combat fighter in USAF service for the next decade or two. It is in the areas of weapons and sensor capability updates that the United States will have to rely upon in challenging the Su-57 for dominance in the air, Russia, of course, expected to reciprocate with future weapon/sensor updates, benefiting from work conducted under the embryonic sixth generation fighter program, studies of which were launched in the second half of the 2010's.

It can be inferred that the AL-41F1 engines installed in the T-50 development aircraft are in a similar thrust category to the derivative AL-41F1-S (117S) engines that powered the Su-35S. However, mid and late production Su-57 aircraft will be powered by the higher thrust Product 30 Stage Two engines. The Su-57 is expected to be capable of supercruise at speeds up to Mach 1.6 (this is circa the maximum speed of the F-35A with afterburner) and in excess of the Mach 1.5 value for the F-22A circulated in USAF (United States Air Force) documentation. In 2021, it cannot be qualified that the Mach 1.6 value for supercruise referred to Su-57 aircraft powered by AL-41F1 engines and may in fact refer to aircraft powered by the Stage Two engines then still under development. What was clear was that the high specific thrust of the engines, combined with the aircraft aerodynamic design, flight control surfaces (including the torque variable engine nozzles) and advanced flight control system, bestowed upon the T-50 a level of manoeuvrability unrivalled by any other fifth generation aircraft, and surpassing that of all other in-service combat aircraft with the possible exception of the Su-35S in some flight regimes.

With the Su-57, Russia has clearly retained its supremacy in aircraft manoeuvrability over her western rivals, although this required certain compromises, such as a slight reduction in low-observability capability, which appears to have been kept at an acceptable level.

In demonstrations, the T-50 (Su-57) certainly lived up to its 'super-manoeuvrability' characterisation, performing such manoeuvres as Pugachev's 'Cobra', 'Bell', 'tail-slide', 'chandelle', 'inside loop' (also referred to as Nestrov's loop' and controlled flat spins to name but a few. From their earliest public demonstrations in the late 1980's, it was clear that the Su-27 possessed manoeuvring capabilities that far exceeded those of its western counterparts. Having previously demonstrated the 'Cobra' and 'Hook' manoeuvres, which clearly demonstrated advances in extreme incidence flight in an operational aircraft, the Russians, in 1996, demonstrated the 'Kulbit' with the Su-37MR equipped with thrust vector control for its engine nozzles. This manoeuvre was basically a 'Cobra' like manoeuvre that, following the high speed run and rapid pitch upwards, more or less to the vertical of the 'Cobra', rather than bringing the nose back down, as in the 'Cobra', the aircraft continued on through the vertical to complete a full rotation around the aircraft lateral axis – in effect an airborne somersault. Another 'Cobra' like manoeuvre saw the aircraft perform a rapid pitch-up to around 130°, maintaining this attitude for some 2-3 seconds whilst rapidly bleeding-off airspeed. The pilot then employed vectored-thrust, pitching the aircraft nose forward before recovering into a dive. Like the 'Cobra' and 'Hook' beforehand, some observers questioned the operational value of such manoeuvres, although the potential in close air combat, particularly in evasion of air to air missiles in the terminal phase, appeared obvious, although only as a last resort as the aircraft inevitably bled energy very rapidly. That said, the T-50 (Su-57), like the Su-27 family, possessed excellent acceleration, being capable of regaining speed very quickly (Harkins, 2015).

T-50-5. Rostec

Page 94-95: A T-50 development aircraft during a 'controlled flat spin' manoeuvre that allowed the aircraft to completely reverse its course within a few seconds. Sukhoi

The 'Bell' manoeuvre could be described as a 'Cobra' manoeuvre where the aircraft, keeping its nose towards the vertical, retained its altitude in the sky, in effect appearing to more or less stand still with its nose more or less at the vertical, around 90° (although it sometimes could pull over to around 100° and beyond), whilst maintaining some forward motion. Coming out of the vertical the pilot would initiate a 180° turn, completely reversing the aircraft original course prior to the commencement of the manoeuvre. When these manoeuvres were conducted by other Russian designed thrust vector controlled aircraft, such as the Su-30SM, these inevitably entered the so called 'tail-slide' as the aircraft lacked the power to hold its altitude in the sky. The Su-35S, with its 117S engines, could hold its altitude and maintain forward motion at speeds of between 120-140 km/h, during such manoeuvres, the Su-57 with higher excess power presumably being capable of same.

Another manoeuvre that could be conducted by the T-50 (Su-57) was a controlled flat spin (also demonstrated by the Su-35S) whereby the pilot retained full control of the aircraft as it conducted a rotating descent. As the Su-57 establishes itself in service there will no doubt be additional extreme agility manoeuvres that come to light. The rapid deceleration caused by many of these extreme manoeuvres could result in a radar breaking lock, which would be useful in avoiding radar guided missiles. Of course, there are other manoeuvres that make the Su-57, like the Su-30MKI/SM and Su-35S, very unpredictable in its flight pattern, an environment that is not ideal for air to air missiles to conduct a successful engagement.

Detractors of the need for super-manoeuvrability in an air superiority aircraft should consider this point: super-manoeuvrability is an additional weapon/defence in the aircraft arsenal/defence suite so long as it does not come at an unacceptable sacrifice in other essential air combat traits, such as speed and altitude performance – sacrifices often associated with aircraft designed with low-observability as a primary driver. In concluding any discussion on super-manoeuvrability it is perhaps pertinent to recount the adage that *it is better to have and not need it than to need it and not have it.*

The fourth development T-50, T-50-4. UAC

The T-50 (Su-57) design team arrived at a well-balanced multifunctional aircraft with low-observability in the radio-electronic and infrared spectrums whilst retaining exceptional aerodynamic/manoeuvring qualities. UAC/NPO Saturn

In 2021, technologies developed and matured for implementation in the Su-57 would feed into future aircraft designs, including the Rostec/Sukhoi Checkmate 5th generation lightweight fighter (top) and Russian sixth generation fighter concepts (bottom). Rostec/Kret

4

ARMAMENT SYSTEMS

The Su-57 has been cleared to carry up to 10000 kg of stores. There has, as of summer 2021, been no official detailed release of the full armament fit for the Su-57. In discussions and interviews, however, information in regards to weapons for initial production aircraft, and weapons in development, currently planned for later production batches, has dripped out at intervals. This, combined with photographs of T-50 development aircraft conducting missile launches from the internal stores bays and carrying weapons on external stores stations, allowed a reasonable detailed picture of the planned weapons fit to be put forward.

The Su-57 was capable of carrying a wide diversity of advanced air to air and air to surface weapons in the two under fuselage internal stores bays – the two shoulder bays for carriage of short-range infrared guided air to air missiles that appeared on United Aircraft Corporation graphics from 2015 appear to have been for illustrative purposes only and do not correspond to actual stores bays. If required, stores could be carried on external stations – at least two on each wing. In addition to the missile/bomb armament the Su-57 was armed with an internal cannon, specifically the the 9A1-4071K rapid fire 30 mm cannon. This weapon, developed for the Su-57 by High Precision Systems, is a modernised variant of the tried and tested GSh-301 30 mm automatic cannon system that armed the Su-27 family of combat aircraft, including the 4th++ generation Su-35S that entered Russian Federation Air Force service in 2014. Flight testing of the 9A1-4071K was conducted on a Su-27SM, with tests of the weapon installed on a T-50 development aircraft commencing in the second half of the 2010's (Harkins, 2015).

It is clear that the current (2021) generation RVV-AE medium range and R-73E short-range air to air missiles could be employed by the Su-57. Replacements for both of these weapons have been in development in the shape of the RVV-SD and RVV-MD respectively. These latter weapons were developed with carriage and launch from internal stores bays in mind. A new long range active radar guided air to air missile, developed under the RVV-BD program, was specified as part of the Su-57 armoury.

The Su-57 was armed with a High Precision Systems 9A1-4071K 30 mm cannon complex housed in the starboard forward fuselage. The cannon port, located below the cockpit, is shown faired over in a T-50 development aircraft (top) and exposed (above). KnAAPO

Series of three stills from a test firing of the High Precision Systems 9A1-4071K rapid fire 30 mm cannon installed on a T-50 ground test rig. UAC

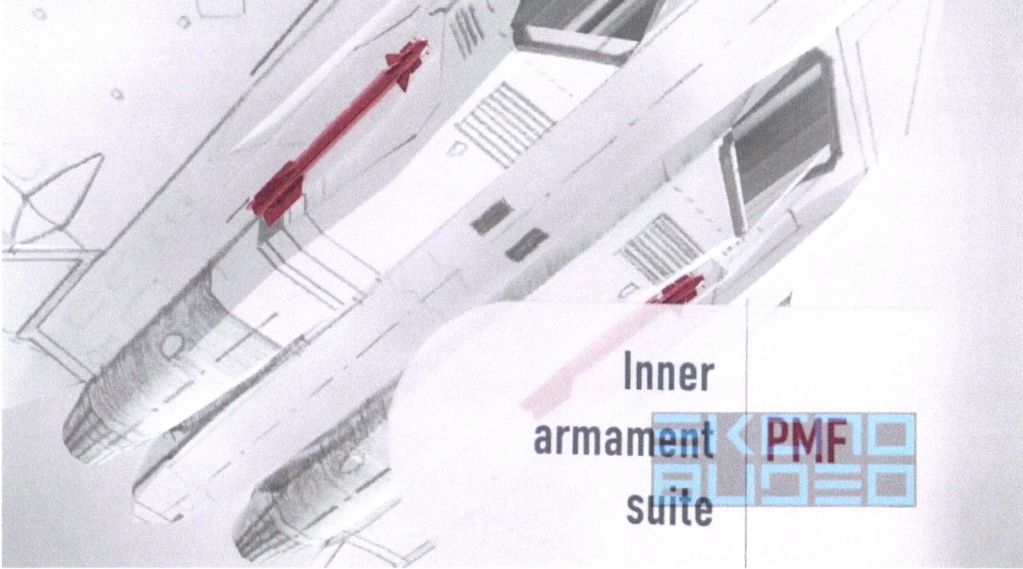

Previous page and this page top: The wide spacing layout of the Su-57 engines allowed incorporation of two spacious under fuselage internal bays for the carriage of stores. This page bottom: Circa 2015, United Aircraft Corporation released graphic material appearing to show two shoulder internal stores bays for the carriage of short range infrared guided air to air missile. This appears to have been for illustrative purposes only. UAC

RVV-BD – Russian studies and developments into long-range air to air missiles in the late 1980's and 1990's was initially aimed at fielding a replacement for the R-33 long-range air to air missile arming the MiG-31 long-range interceptor in Soviet and later Russian Federation Air Force Service. Several studies resulted in a number of designations being applied to various programs, including R-37 and K-172, but the service weapon was apparently developed under the wider RVV-BD program.

In 2009, Russia and India had entered into talks on developing an ultra-long-range air to air missile under the designation R-172, which was then under development by Russian Design House Novator. This weapon was intended for attacking high value targets, such as airborne refuelling tankers and airborne warning and control system aircraft like the Boeing E-3 Sentry, in service with NATO (North Atlantic Treaty Organisation) nations. Mock-ups of the long-range air to air missile were shown on the inner wing stations of the first Su-35S development aircraft. However, for Russian domestic service, the replacement for the R-33 on the updated MiG-31BM was allocated to JSC GosMKB Vympel, State Machine Building Design Bureau, for full development, this yielding the RVV-BD.

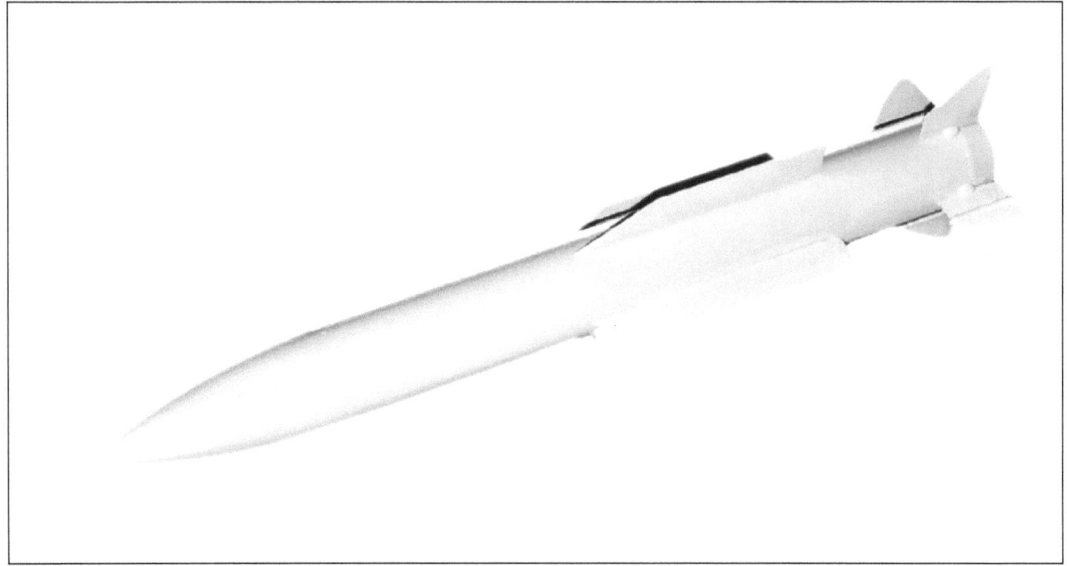

RVV-BD long-rang air to air missile. Vympel MKB

The resultant RVV-BD emerged as a new generation long-range air to air missile, surpassing the operational parameters of the R-33 in Russian service. The RVV-BD would be capable of engaging the full-spectrum of airborne targets – high performance tactical combat aircraft at subsonic and supersonic speeds, long-range heavy bomber/missile carrier aircraft, transport aircraft, support aircraft, helicopters and cruise missiles etc. The missile, which operated on a multi-channel fire and forget basis, could operate in day/night and adverse weather conditions, in an high density electronic jamming environment at all-aspect angles, against background clutter generated by Earth's land and water surfaces (TMC).

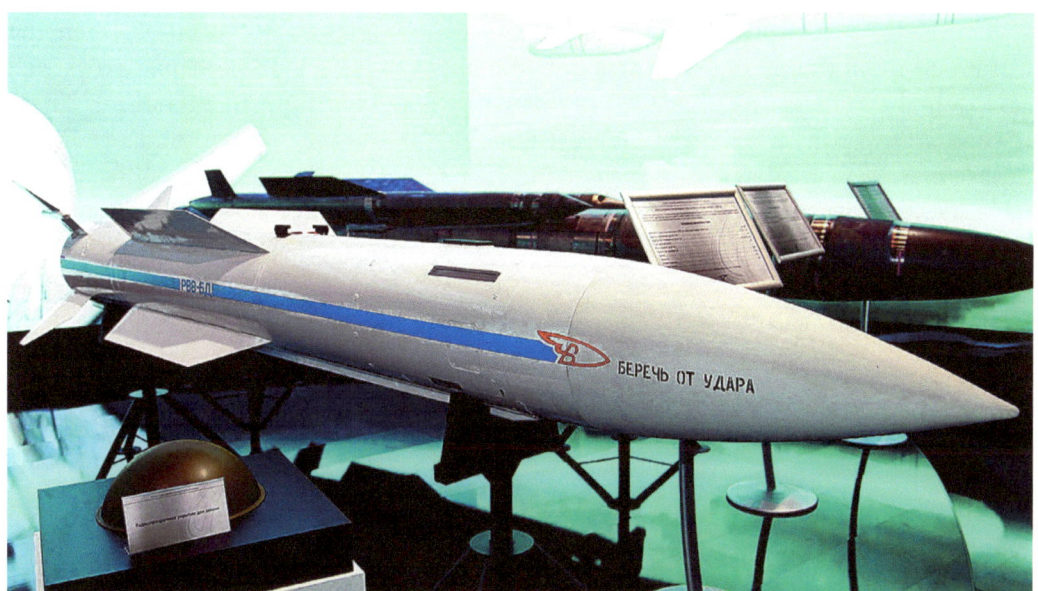

The RVV-BD active radar guided long-range air to air missile could engage the full-spectrum of air to air targets at ranges out to several hundred kilometres. Vympel MKB

The RVV-BD was powered by a single dual-mode solid propellant rocket motor, ignition occurring once the missile had been ejected away from the launch platform. Depending on launch platform configuration, the RVV-BD was launched from an AKY-410-1 or AKY-620 launcher/ejector. Once launched, the weapon would fly to the target area under inertial guidance, receiving course updates through data-link, with active radar homing in the terminal phase of the engagement. The target would be destroyed by a powerful high explosive blast fragmentation warhead activated by either an active radar proximity or impact fuse (TMC).

If the RVV-BD formed a primary air to air armament for the Su-57, then the maximum number that may be carried would likely be four, with perhaps two carried on external wing stations (this is an estimate and may be subject to alteration). There is contention about whether the RVV-BD could be routinely accommodated in the Su-57 internal stores bays. Other than the 1.02 m tail fin span and width (the latter have identical values) the RVV-BD is smaller than the internal carriage optimised Kh-58UShKE, therefore, routine internal carriage could be facilitated if required.

Vympel MKB RVV-BD – data furnished by Tactical Missiles Corporation

Length: 4.05 m
Diameter: 0.38 m
Wingspan: 0.72 m
Fin span: 1.02 m
Launch weight: not more than 510 kg
Warhead weight: 60 kg
Maximum launch range against targets in forward hemisphere: up to 200 km (value is for the export standard. No officially sanctioned value has been released for the variant in domestic Russian service – TASS news agency reports a range of 300 km

---

As noted above, the Su-57 could be armed with the standard Russian medium and short-range air to air weapons – Vympel (TMC) RVV-AE (K-77) – NATO reporting name AA-12 'Adder' – medium range active radar guided missile and R-73E (K-73E) short-range infrared guided missile and their updated developments, the RVV-MD and RVV-SD.

RVV-AE – Despite the emergence in the early 1990's of the RVV-AE, development of which apparently commenced in earnest in 1982, this weapon was not hurriedly adopted into widespread Russian Federation Air Force service due to insufficient funding attributed to the economic woes that befell Russia following the break-up of the former Soviet Union. The weapon was, however, thought to have entered limited trials service in Russia in 1994, and over the ensuing two decades or so was integrated onto the full-range of Russian designed $4^{th}+$, $4^{th}++$ and fifth generation strike fighter aircraft designs – specifically MiG-29M/K/35/D Unified Family, the Su-30 series, Su-34, Su-35S and tested on the T-50 (Su-57).

The RVV-AE, which was exported to a number of nations, emerged with narrow-span wings of rectangular shape and four lattice control surfaces at the rear. Among the benefits of this type of control surface included reduced flow-separation at high angle of attack. Like its western analogues, the American AIM-120 Advanced Medium Range Air to Air Missile and the European MICA EM active radar guided air to air missile, the RVV-AE could be employed in a launch-and-forget mode and featured a multi-stage guidance system that included inertial in the initial phase with mid-course updates via an aircraft to missile data-link for longer range engagements, with active radar homing in the terminal phase of the missiles flight to the target. The missiles on-board active-radar apparently had an acquisition-range in the region of 20 km (Harkins, 2015).

The RVV-AE was adopted as the baseline medium range air to air missile arming advanced variants of the Su-27 series – Su-30SM and Su-35S etc. – and may form an element of the primary armoury of the Su-57. Vympel MKB/Author

Vympel MKB noted that whilst the RVV-AE was heavier than the AIM-120A and MICA EM, the Russian missile had longer range and better performance when engaging manoeuvring targets compared to its western rivals. The RVV-AE had a minimum engagement range of 0.3 km in the rear hemisphere and a maximum range of 80 km in the forward hemisphere, apparently reached speeds of Mach 4 and could engage targets manoeuvring at up to 12 g at altitudes of 0.2 to 25 km. The missile, which featured an active-radar fuse for the 22.5 kg class warhead, could also apparently be employed in a self-defence mode to intercept missiles launched at the host aircraft, although such a capability would of course depend upon the ability of the on-board radar to detect the incoming missile (Harkins, 2015).

Vympel MKB RVV-AE (R-77) – data furnished by Tactical Missiles Corporation

Propulsion: solid propellant rocket motor
Length: 3.6 m
Diameter: 0.2 m
Wingspan: 0.4 m
Control plane span: 0.7 m in flight position
Launch weight: 175 kg
Speed: Mach 4 class
Range: minimum 0.3 km in rear hemisphere and maximum 80 km in front hemisphere
Engagement altitude: 0.2 to 25 km
Warhead: 22.5 kg class high explosive
Fuse: active-radar
Guidance: inertial, command and active-radar in the terminal phase

RVV-SD medium range air to air missile. TMC/Vympel MKB

RVV-SD – The improved RVV-AE, referred to as K-77M, appeared to be a separate program from the RVV-SD developed by Vympel MKB. The RVV-SD, described by Tactical Missiles Corporation as an active radar guided medium range air to air missile, was formally unveiled in 2009 as a replacement for the RVV-AE. Clearly an evolution of the latter missile, the RVV-SD incorporated a number of improvements over its forebear – longer engagement range, increased overall engagement capability and enhanced resistance to electronic countermeasures. Tactical Missiles Corporation described the missile as 'intended for hitting air targets (fighters, bombers, attack aircraft, helicopters… cruise missiles) day and night, at all angles, under electronic countermeasures, on background of earth and water surfaces, including multichannel application fire-and-forget' (TMC). The missile, powered by a single mode rocket engine, incorporated inertial homing in the initial phase of flight, with course corrected radar updates and terminal phase active radar homing. The target would destroyed by a rod-shaped multi-charge warhead with detonation by a laser non-contact target sensor (TMC).

For external carriage on 4th, 4th+, 4th++ and fifth generation aircraft the missile is carried on and launched from the AKU-170E missile ejection launcher. The weapon dimensions are well within the parameters for accommodation in the Su-57 internal stores bays and footage of RVV-AE/SD launches from the T-50 internal weapon bays suggest that the standard missiles are accommodated and launched without issue.

RVV-SD launched from a Sukhoi Su-27 series derivative during development testing. TMC

Vympel MKB RVV-SD – data furnished by Tactical Missiles Corporation and Vympel MKB

Length: 3.71 m
Diameter: 0.2 m
Wingspan: 0.42 m
Rudder span: 0.68 m
Launch weight: 190 kg
Minimum launch range: minimum 0.3 km in the rear hemisphere
Maximum launch range: up to 110 km in forward the hemisphere
Engagement altitude: 0.2 to 25 km

Series of stills showing an RVV-AE/SD launch from the forward fuselage weapons bay of a T-50 development aircraft.

When it entered service in the 1980's, the R-73 was probably the most advanced short-range infrared guided air to air missile in the world, being a generation ahead of the latest variants of the American AIM-9L/M Sidewinder or European Magic 2 short-range infrared guided air to air missiles then arming NATO fighters. Only in the early twenty first century did western nations field comparable systems in the shape of the Matra British Aerospace Dynamics Alenia Advanced Short Range Air to Air Missile and Raytheon AIM-9X Evolved Sidewinder (Harkins, 2015).

The R-73 was developed with high agility as a design driver, augmented by the ability of the pilot of Su-27 or MiG-29 fighter aircraft to cue the weapon to targets at up to 60° off-boresight via a helmet mounted sight system. High manoeuvrability was achieved by a combination of a number of factors, including incorporation of four forward control fins, elevators attached to the rear fins, which were fixed, and deflector vanes positioned in the nozzle of the rocket engine (Harkins, 2015).

The R-73E had a longer reach than most western analogues, such as the many AIM-9 variants. Confirmed minimum engagement range against a tail-on target was 0.3 km and maximum range was 30 km against a head-on target, with the capability of engaging targets manoeuvring at loads up to 12 g (Harkins, 2015).

Vympel MKB R-73E – data furnished by TMC and Vympel MKB

Propulsion: solid propellant rocket motor
Length: 2.9 m
Diameter: 0.17 m
Span: 0.51 m fin span and 0.38 m control plane span
Launch weight: 105 kg
Range: 30 km maximum head on and 0.3 km minimum tail on against up to 12 g manoeuvring targets
Engagement altitude: from 0.02 to 20 km
Warhead: 8 kg high explosive expanding rod
Guidance: all-aspect passive infrared

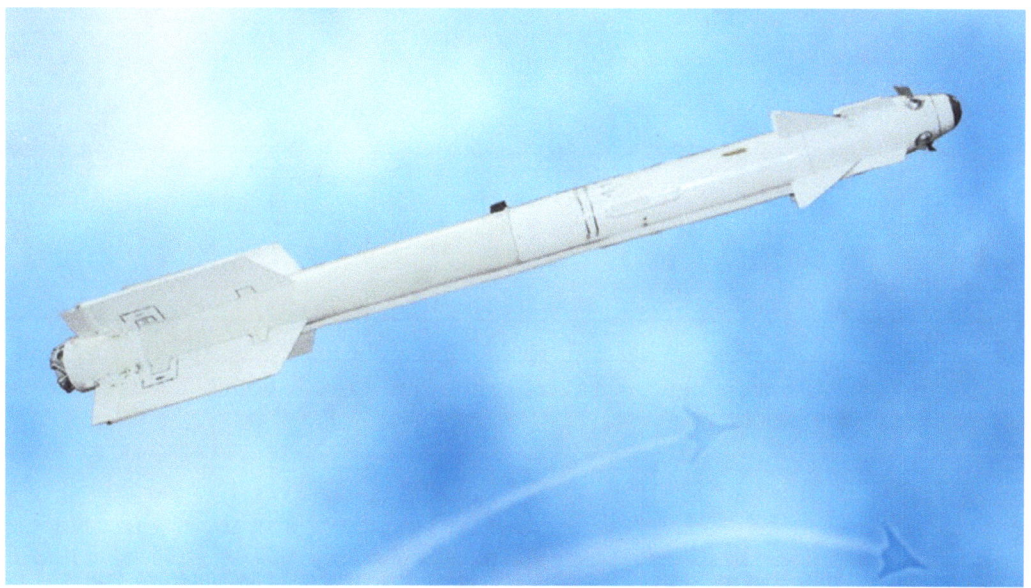

R-73E short-range air to air missile. TMC

Top: R-73E infrared guided air to air missile external carriage on a MiG AT light combat aircraft demonstrator. Bottom: Rear sections of an R-73E showing the rear wings and thrust-vector control vanes, which bestowed upon the missile its exceptional agility. Author

RVV-MD – An evolution of the R-73, the RVV-MD emerged as a new generation highly agile infrared guided missile developed to arm the new generation of Russian 4th+, 4th++ and fifth generation fighter aircraft. The Vympel description stated the 'short range missile for close high manoeuvrable air combat provides hitting air targets (fighters, bombers, combat aircrafts, military aircrafts and

112

helicopters), day and night, at all angles, on background of earth, under active enemy counteraction' (Vympel MKB). The missile, powered by a single mode engine, featured enhanced anti-jamming protection over its forebear, including optical jamming, and was capable of 'all angles passive infrared target homing (double range individual homing) with combined aero-gas dynamics control' (TMC). The target would be destroyed by a rod-shaped warhead activated by a laser non-contact sensor fuse in the RVV-MDL variant or a radio non-contact sensor in the RVV-MD. On Sukhoi and MiG fighter aircraft the weapon was carried on and launched from the P-72-1D (P-72-1BD2) type rail tracked launcher. The RVV-MD could be carried in the Su-57 internal weapon bays and on underwing external stores stations.

RVV-MD short-range air to air missile. TMC

Vympel MKB RVV-MD – data furnished by TMC and Vympel MKB

Length: 2.92 m
Diameter: 0.17 m
Wingspan: 0.51 m
Rudder span: 0.385 m
Launch weight: 106 kg
Launch range: front hemisphere, up to 40 km and minimum in rear hemisphere, 0.3 km
Target designation angles: ± 60°
Homing head coordinator deviation spheres: ± 75°
Engagement altitude: can engage targets flying at 0.02 to 20 km
Overload of target: can engage targets manoeuvring at up to 12 *g*
Warhead weight: 8 kg high explosive

Page 114-115: Series of stills of an R-73E/RVV-MD launch from a starboard external stores station of a T-50 steep climb. UAC

In 2021, air to surfaces weapons specified for carriage by the Su-57 included the Kh-58UShKE (X-58UShKE), Kh-38ME (X-38ME), Kh-35UE (X-35UE), the Grom-E1 missile, Grom-E2 glide bomb, KAB-500S and KAB-250LG corrected air bombs and a hypersonic missile then under development. Other weapons may be specified at a later date or for exported.

Kh-58UShKE – Developed with suppressed dimensions for internal carriage in the Su-57 weapons bays, JSC Raduga State Engineering Design Bureau developed the Kh-58UShKE as the standard anti-radiation (anti-radar) weapon for the Su-57. As well as internal carriage, this weapon could be carried on at least two of the external stores stations if required – this was confirmed by the developer whom stated that the missile can be launched from 'supressed fuselage suspension' (internal) (TMC). When carried internally the missile would be launched from the UVKU-50 ejection system, or from the AKU-58 ejection system – incorporated a target designation system – for external carriage. The Kh-58UShKE, which could be fitted with a range of passive radar homing heads (A, A1, B, B1, C) and featured an automatic control platform free navigation system, could target and destroy ground based radar systems emitting on the 1.2 to 11. Gigahertz frequency and operated in a 'continuous emitting mode with range A' (TMC). Missile operating parameters included a maximum range of 245 km when launched from 20000 m altitude, the missile having a flight speed of 4200 km/h when nearing the target, which would be destroyed by the 149 kg high explosive warhead (TMC).

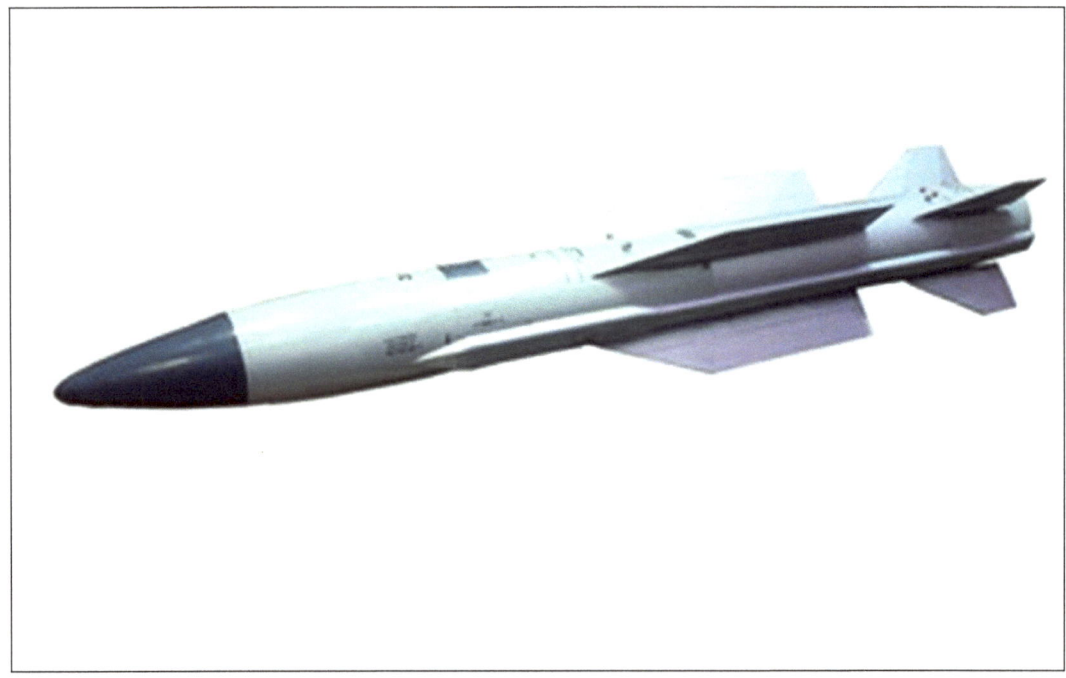

The Raduga developed Kh-58UShKE (X-58UShKE) anti-radiation missile was developed for carriage in the confines of the Su-57 internal stores bays. The missile bestowed upon the host platform the ability to strike threat radar systems at ranges out to 245 km, assuming launch from an altitude of 20000 m. UAC

Kh-58UShKE – data furnished by Tactical Missiles Corporation

Launch altitude envelope: 0.2 km up to carrier platform operational altitude
Carrier launch speed envelope when released from external stores station: Mach 0.47-Mach 1.5
Maximum launch range (carrier flight parameters H=0-200 m: 76-245 km
Minimum range when launched at altitude of 0-200 m: 10-12 km
Target aspect on launch: ±15°
Maximum flight speed: 4200 km/h
Control system: SNAU based on BINS+ShPRGS
Hit probability for a 20 m radius with the radar target located in the centre: 0.8
Warhead type and weight: High explosive, 149 kg
Missile launch weight: 650 kg
Length: 4.19 m
Width: 0.4 m
Height: 0.4 m
Wingspan: 0.8 m
Diameter: 0.38 m

Kh-35UE anti-ship missile. TMC

Kh-35UE – The Kh-35UE was the baseline anti-ship missile specified for the Su-57. This missile, which was an evolution of the Kh-35E, was designed to destroy surface vessels, including warships displacing up to 5,000 tonnes. Once launched from the mother aircraft the missile would descend to an altitude of some 10-15 m above the sea surface, dropping to 4 m for the terminal phase of the flight, to strike targets in sea states up to 6 in an active electronic countermeasures environment. The ARGS-35EU active radar seeker had an acquisition range of around 20 km, thereafter the target was locked-on (TMC, Harkins, 2015).

The Kh-35UE improved on the Kh-35E in a number of areas, including range, which was doubled from 130 km to 260 km, and the missile featured an improved post-launch horizontal turn capability (TMC, Harkins, 2015).

> Kh-35UE – data furnished by Tactical Missiles Corporation
>
> Launch range envelope: 7-260 km
> Missile flight altitude over wave ridge: 10-15 m en-route to target area, dropping to about 4 m in the terminal phase of the flight
> Missile cruise speed: Mach 0.8 to 0.85
> Missile turn angle in horizontal plane post launch: ± 130°
> Guidance system: inertial plus satellite navigation plus active-passive radio homing head
> Maximum range of passive detection and locking with active-passive radio homing head: 50 km
> Launch weight: 550 kg for aircraft launched variant (helicopter and ship launched variants were 650 and 670 kg respectively)
> Warhead: 145 kg penetrating high explosive fragmentation
> Length: 3.85 m for aircraft launched variant (ship/land launched variants are 4.4 m)
> Body diameter: 0.42 m
> Wing span: 1.33 m
> Weather conditions for use: any sea conditions up to sea state 6

Kh-38ME – The baseline battlefield support missile specified for the Su-57 was the Kh-38ME family of air launched missiles – Kh-38MAE, Kh-38MKE, Kh-38MLE and Kh-38MTE – optimised to destroy battlefield targets ranging from soft targets to reinforced targets and armoured vehicles. The Kh-38ME series could also be employed against sea surface targets. The main difference in the variants of the missile were in payload and guidance – Kh-38MAE with inertial plus active radar guidance; Kh-38MKE with inertial plus satellite guidance; Kh-38MLE with inertial plus semi-active laser guidance and the Kh-38MTE with inertial plus thermal imaging guidance. All variants were armed with a 250 kg high explosive fragmentation warhead except the Kh-38MKE, which was fitted with a cluster munitions warhead (TMC).

Kh-38ME short-range battlefield air to surface missile. TMC

Kh-38ME – data furnished by Tactical Missiles Corporation

Launch range envelope: 3-40 km
Launch speed: Mach 2.2 maximum
Launch range: 200-12000 m
Missile turn angle in horizontal plane after launch: ±80°
Target destruction probability: 0.8
Maximum launch weight: 520 kg
Warhead weight: up to 250 kg
Fuse type: contact
Motor type: two-phase solid-propellant motor
Length: 4.2 m
Body diameter: 0.31 m
Wing span: 1.14 m

For air to surface missions, the Su-57 could be armed with the GROM-E1 air to surface guided missile and the GROM-E2 air to surface glide-bomb unit. The GROM-E1 guided missile was developed by Tactical Missiles Corporation to strike fixed coordinate surface targets day or night in environmental conditions of fair or adverse weather at ranges out to 120 km. The missile was guided to the target by an inertial guidance system that incorporated a complex for jam-resistant receipt of satellite navigation signals. The target would be destroyed or disabled through the fragmentation/blast warhead (TMC).

GROM-E1 – data furnished by Tactical Missiles Corporation

Maximum launch range: 120 km
Minimum launch range: 0-10 km depending upon release altitude
Launch altitude range: 0.5 to 12 km
Launch speed: up to Mach 1.5
Gross launch weight: 600 kg
Target locating angle in horizontal plane: up to ±180°
Warhead weight: 315 kg
Length: 4.2 m
Missile body diameter: 0.31 m
Wingspan: 1.9 m

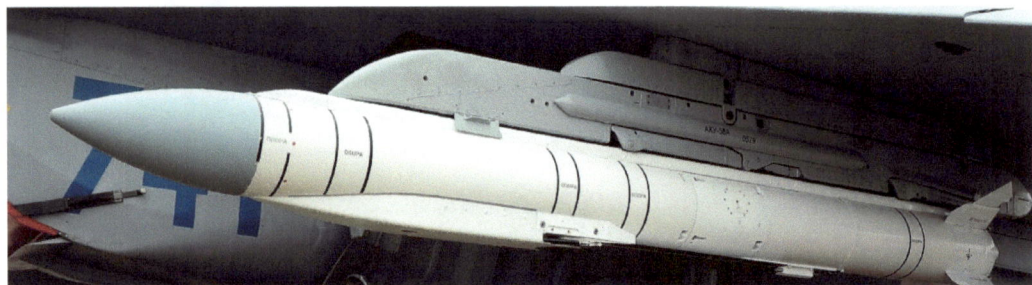

The GROM-E1 guided missile and GROM-E2 guided glide bomb unit constituted a new generation of precision strike weapons to arm Russian 4th+/4th++ and fifth generation strike fighters. TMC

The GROM-E2 glide-bomb was developed by Tactical Missiles Corporation to strike fixed coordinate targets day or night in environmental conditions of fair or adverse weather at ranges out to 50 km. The bomb would glide to the target under guidance of an inertial navigation system that incorporated a complex for jam-resistant receipt of satellite navigation signals. The target would be destroyed or disabled by the powerful fragmentation and blast warheads (TMC).

GROM-E2 – data furnished by Tactical Missiles Corporation

Maximum launch range: 50 km
Minimum launch range: 0-10 km
Launch altitude range: 0.5 to 12 km
Launch speed: up to Mach 1.5
Gross launch weight: 598 kg
Target locating angle in horizontal plane: up to ±180°
Warhead weight: 315+165 kg
Length: 4.2 m
Missile body diameter: 0.31 m
Wingspan: 1.9 m

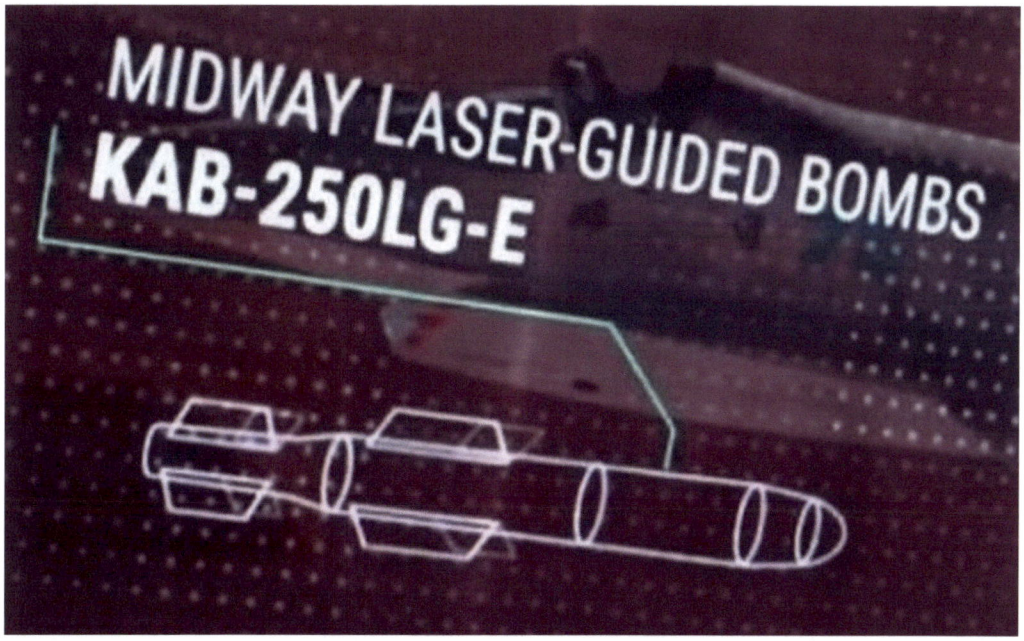

Graphic depicting the KAB-250LG-E midway laser guided (corrected trajectory) guided bomb unit designed for internal carriage in the Su-57 and Checkmate 5th generation multidimensional fighter aircraft. UAC-Rostec

Under current planning the Su-57 would be capable of operating with a number of corrected (guided) bomb units, including the KAB-250 and KAB-500 families (specific variants appear to be the KAB-250LG and KAB-500S), the former being designed for accommodation in the Su-57 internal stores bays. It is unclear how many of these weapons could be carried, however, it will likely be less than the 8 of each type that can be carried externally by the Su-35S.

The GNPP Region developed KAB-500S-E Corrected Air Bomb, equipped with a satellite navigation system, can be employed to attack fixed coordinate surface targets in environmental conditions of fair and adverse weather day or night (TMC).

KAB-500S-E Corrected Air Bomb – data furnished by Tactical Missiles Corporation
Launch weight: 560 kg Warhead explosive weight: 195 kg Length: 3.0 m Diameter: 0.4 m Wingspan of stabilisers: 0.75 m Release altitude: 0.5-5 km Carrier launch speed: 550-1100 km/h Aiming accuracy (Root mean square deviation): 7-12 m Warhead type: high explosive Fuse: Contact with three delay settings

KAB-500S-E Correct Air Bomb. TMC

Other variants of the KAB-500 family, such as the KAB-500Kr and KAB-500-OD, may be carried on external wing stations, but there is no indication that the larger KAB-1500 would be accommodated. Other armament options could include the Kh-31AD supersonic anti-ship cruise missile – Kh-31 series missile were trialled on T-50 external stores stations during development testing.

As Russia progresses with the introduction of advanced hypersonic cruise missiles on surface, sub-surface and airborne platforms, planning as at 2021 called for the Su-57 to be armed with such a weapon. This missile, development of which was funded under the Russian state armament program for 2018-2027 and embodying studies for the Kh-95 long-range hypersonic weapon (it is unclear in 2021 if the Kh-95 would form the basis of the hypersonic missile intended to arm the Su-57), would likely be smaller in overall dimensions by comparison to the Kinzhal hypersonic cruise missile carried by the MiG-31K.

5

T-50 FLIGHT TESTING TO SU-57 SERIAL PRODUCTION

During the T-50 flight development program the various trials aircraft were put through the full range of test procedures required for a fifth generation tactical combat aircraft – included the full-spectrum of aerodynamic evaluation, complementing ground tests, aircraft stability, control and dynamic robustness, along with testing of aircraft equipment and systems. By early 2014, super-manoeuvrability flight testing was well advanced, demonstrating the T-50 designs superiority in this particular realm in comparison to western analogues (Harkins, 2015).

When the T-50 was unveiled in June 2010, the then Russian Federation Deputy Defence Minister, Vladimir Popovkin, stated, under a draft armament program covering the period up to 2010 that more than 50 T-50 PAK FA (Perspective Aviation Complex for Frontline Aviation) aircraft were to be acquired from 2016. Ambitiously, the Russian President had stated that a batch of development/pre-series production T-50 should be delivered to the Russian Federation Air Force test centre in Lipetsk for test and evaluation in 2013, to be followed by delivery of series production standard aircraft to operational units in 2015. This schedule was, at best, unrealistic, the first serial produced Su-57 (T-50 aircraft were formally designated Su-57 in December 2017) eventually being delivered to the Russian Aerospace Forces in December 2020.

Its public perception still little more than a rumour, with few hard facts available, the first of the prototype T-50 aircraft, T-50-1, conducted its maiden flight on 29 January 2010, when Sukhoi test pilot Sergey Bogdan lifted the aircraft off the runway at Komsomolsk-on-Amur at 11.19 am. This flight, which lasted 47 minutes, was chaperoned by a Sukhoi Su-27UB chase aircraft (Harkins, 2015).

The test/development program would involve nine flight test aircraft and no less than three ground test airframes. Construction of the first flight prototype had commenced in 2007, along with two of the ground test articles, one of which was utilised as a 'complex ground stand' and the other used for static tests (Sukhoi). The static test aircraft, apparently initially referred to as the T-50-0, but later revealed as the T-50KPO, was completed in summer 2009, by which time three T-50 flight prototypes were under construction. The other ground test airframe, the T-50-KN (later KNS), was, in effect, an integrated systems testbed for ground testing of various systems, including engines, flight control system and later the AFAR (Active Phased Array Radar) complex. This non-flight rated test-bed apparently commenced ground tests with AL-41F1 engines at Komsomolsk-on-Amur in autumn 2009, apparently conducting taxi test runs with Sergey Bogdan at the controls on 23 December that year (Harkins, 2015).

A pair of Su-57 development aircraft break port and starboard during a demonstration/development flight. UAC

Runway taxi test runs with T-50-1 apparently commenced on 21 January 2010, in preparation for the first flight just over one week later. January 21st also apparently saw the commencement of flight tests of the Su-27M, Article 710, with an AL-41F1 engine installed in one of its engine bays in place of the standard AL-31F. The flight test of the AL-41F1 on the Su-27M took place at the M.M Gromov Flight Research Institute, Zhukovsky, Moscow, to clear the way for the maiden flight of the T-50-1, powered by two such engines. T-50-1 conducted a further series of runway taxi test runs – high and low speed – on 23 January 2010, during which the pilot (Bogdan) took the aircraft close to take-off speed prior to deploying the drogue parachute to aid deceleration (Harkins, 2015).

During the T-50-1 maiden flight on 29 January 2010 (the intention of flying T-50-1 in 2009 was missed by less than one calendar month), several tests were conducted, including cycling the undercarriage through retraction and extraction, check out of basic engine performance parameters, aircraft controllability and operation of primary systems. Bogdan commented that T-50-1 had proven to be 'easy and comfortable to pilot', having successfully completed all planned tests. T-50-1's second flight apparently took place on 12 February 2010, by which time the aircraft had been painted in a multi-grey/blueish scheme. The third flight was apparently conducted the following day. Between 29 January and 26 March 2010, T-50-1 apparently flew six times in order to clear the preliminary flight acceptance, following which the aircraft was grounded for updates and maintenance (Harkins, 2015).

The T-50 prototype, T-50-1, underwent engine testing on 20 December 2009 (top) and conducted taxi trial runs on 23 January 2010 (bottom). Sukhoi

Su-57

Page 126-128: Series of photographs of the T-50-1 maiden flight. Sukhoi

On 8 April 2010, T-50-1, along with the avionics testbed, T-50-KNS, which had been employed to verify avionics performance prior to the T-50-1 maiden flight, was delivered to the Sukhoi facility at Zhukovsky aboard an Antonov An-124 Ruslan transport aircraft. A program of preliminary tests of aircraft components, strength, and avionics systems was conducted prior to the re-commencement of flight testing on 29 April 2010, this apparently being T-50-1's seventh flight. T-50-1 was demonstrated to the Russian Prime Minister on 17 June 2010. By the 23rd of that month, the aircraft had conducted 16 flights (Harkins, 2015).

T-50-1 during its second flight, apparently on 12 February 2010. Sukhoi

Following a two-month grounding for maintenance and updates to be incorporated, T-50-1 resumed flying in mid-August 2010. On the last day of that month the aircraft, flown by Bogdan, was demonstrated to a delegation from the Republic of India that was in Russia for talks on the progress of the Indo/Russian FGFA (Fifth Generation Fighter Aircraft) program potentially to be developed from the T-50 for the Indian Air Force.

In September 2010, the pool of test pilots for the T-50 test program was increased, Roman Kondratyev flying T-50-1 on the 15th of the month, followed by Yury Vashchuk on the 20th. Following a further grounding for installation of updates from late autumn 2010, T-50-1 resumed flying from Zhukovsky on 10 February 2011 – the aircraft exceeded the speed of sound for the first time during an envelope expansion flight on 9 March that year. In March 2011, the second flight development aircraft, T-50-2, had joined the flight test program when this aircraft conducted its 44 minute maiden flight on 3rd of the month (pilot, Sergey Bogdan). Acceptance testing of T-50-2 was completed at Komsomolsk-on-Amur following completion of four flights, all conducted by Bogdan between the 3rd and 5th of March. The aircraft was then painted as it was prepared to be transferred to Zhukovsky, where it arrived aboard an An-124 on 3 April 2011 (Harkins, 2015).

The second T-50 development aircraft, T-50-2, ground operations for its maiden flight on 3 March 2011. Sukhoi

The second T-50 development aircraft, T-50-2, during and taxiing at the end of its maiden flight on 3 March 2011. Sukhoi

The new Russian fifth generation fighter had its public debut when T-50-2 was displayed at the MAKS-2011 trade show in August 2011. T-50-2 lifts-off for its display (top) and gains altitude on the climb-out (bottom). Sukhoi

The third flight development aircraft, T-50-3, conducted its maiden flight on 22 November 2011 (pilot, Sergey Bogdan) – the aircraft was airborne for just over one hour. This aircraft was used to flight test a prototype AFAR radar complex, such tests commencing in August 2012 (Kret). Sukhoi revealed on the 8th of that month that air to air and air to surface modes were evaluated during the flight tests. A ground test-phase with the AFAR radar complex installed was also conducted (Harkins, 2015).

Page 133: T-50-2 in formation with a Sukhoi Su-34 and Su-35S at MAKS 2011 – August 2011 (top) and the third T-50 development aircraft, T-50-3, lifts-off from Komsomolsk-on-Amur on its maiden flight on 22 November 2011 (bottom). Page 134: The undercarriage is retracted on T-50-3 during its maiden flight on 22 November 2011. Page 135: T-50-3 lands at the conclusion of its maiden flight on 22 November 2011. Sukhoi/KnAAPO

Other test points conducted during August 2012 included in-flight refuelling docking trials between a development T-50 and an Ilyushin Il-78 in-flight refuelling tanker aircraft, in company with a Sukhoi Su-25UB 'Frogfoot' tactical combat aircraft. At this time, T-50-2 was involved in testing of stability and controllability in a number of configurations in both subsonic and supersonic flight regimes, whilst T-50-1 had completed a flight program studying 'large supercritical angles of attack and manoeuvrability' (Sukhoi).

The fourth flight development aircraft, T-50-4 take-off from Komsomolsk-on-Amur on its maiden flight on 12 December 2012. KnAAPO

The fourth flight development aircraft, T-50-4, during its maiden flight on 12 December 2012 (top) and landing at Komsomolsk-on-Amur (bottom). KnAAPO

The fourth T-50 development aircraft, T-50-4, lands at Komsomolsk-on-Amur at the conclusion of its maiden flight on 12 December 2012. KnAAPO

T-50-4 deploys and jettisons its drogue parachute assembly during the landing run at Komsomolsk-on-Amur following its maiden flight on 12 December 2012. KnAAPO

The fourth flight development aircraft, T-50-4, conducted its 40 minute maiden flight from Komsomolsk-on-Amur on 12 December 2012 (pilot, Sergey Bogdan). This aircraft was flown by Bogdan from Komsomolsk-on-Amur to Zhukovsky, with several stopovers, on 18 January 2013. As the flight test program ramped up, a Russian Federation Air Force pilot, apparently Colonel Rafael Suleimanov, a test pilot at the Russian State Flight Test Centre, made that services first flight in a T-50, lifting off from Zhukovsky on 25 April 2013 (Harkins, 2015).

Page 140-141: T-50-4 maiden flight, 12 December 2012. KnAAPO

Following its debut at the 2011 MAKS show at Zhukovsky, the T-50 again took centre stage when it was demonstrated at MAKS-2013 on 27 August 2013. A T-50 was flown in a solo demonstration, as it had been in 2011 (pilot, Sergey Bogdan). MAKS-2013 also included multi-ship demonstrations involving T-50-1, T-50-2 and T-50-4 (Harkins, 2015).

Three ship formation of T-50-1, T-50-2 and T-50-4 at MAKS-2013, 27 August 2013. Sukhoi

T-50-4 at MAKS-2013 on 1 September 2013.

T-50-1 and T-50-4 in formation at MAKS-2013 on 1 September 2013. Sukhoi

The year 2013 also saw the maiden flight of the fifth flight development aircraft when T-50-5 lifted off from Komsomolsk-on-Amur on 27 October (conflicting documentation states 28 October) that year (pilot, Roman Kondratyev). There were no problems encountered during the 50 minute flight, which included testing of the engines and aircraft stability. T-50-5 conducted a short flight-test phase at Komsomolsk-on-Amur before flying to the Gromov Flight Research Institute, Zhukovsky, on 20 November 2013 (pilot, Yuri Vashchuk), joining the other four development aircraft after a journey that included three stopovers (Harkins, 2015).

On 21 February 2014, T-50-2 was flown by Pilot 1st Class Sergey Chernyshev to join the 929th Chkalov State Flight Test Centre at Akhtubinsk, southern Russia, to participate in Joint State Tests. This aircraft then became the first of the T-50 prototypes to be fully integrated into the state test program, the aircraft being joined later in 2014 by T-50-3 and T-50-4. In late May that year, these latter two aircraft conducted demonstration flights under the auspices of the Russian Aviadarts air combat skill competition. The flights, staged at the Pogonovo proving ground in Voronezh Region, Russia, were conducted by Sergey Bogdan and Roman Kondratyev. The aircraft conducted a number of low-altitude manoeuvres configured with underwing stores - a pair each of RVV-AE/SD and R-73E air to air missiles in the case of T-50-3 and a pair each of RVV-AE/SD and Kh-31 missiles in the case of T-50-4 (Harkins, 2015).

Page 146-148: The fifth flight development T-50, T-50-5, conducted its maiden flight on **27 October 2013.** Knaaz

T-50-5 approaches for landing during its maiden flight on 27 October 2013, with a Sukhoi Su-30M2 flying chase (top) and on touch down at the conclusion of the flight (bottom). Knaaz

Page 150: T-50-5 lines-up for take-off (top) and during a development flight (bottom). Page 151: T-50-5 during a development flight, circa 2014 (top) and T-50-5 following a landing accident on 10 June 2014 (bottom). KnAAPO

On 10 June 2014, the program suffered a setback when T-50-5 caught fire whilst landing after a test flight. The Sukhoi statement read: "Today after the regular test flight of the T-50 aircraft at the airfield of the M.M. Gromov Flight Research Institute in Zhukovsky near Moscow, while the plane was landing, a smoke above the right air intake was observed, then a local fire broke out. The fire was quickly extinguished. The plane is to be repaired. There were no injuries" (Sukhoi).

The damage to the aircraft was repairable and T-50-5 re-joined the flight test program under the designation T-50-5P on 16 October 2015. In January that year, Rostec Corporation stated that there were eight aircraft either built or in construction, including the five flying prototypes. It was unclear at that time if this referred to flight rated examples or if those figures included the ground test airframes, a third example of which had been delivered in December 2014 for static and endurance testing. In addition, an avionics test stand HIL (MTA) was commissioned around March 2013. The function of this stand was primarily the ground based integration of T-50 avionics systems. A sled-test rig had been employed to verify the pilot ejection seat system prior to the commencement of flight testing. Over the next few years, it became clear that the test aircraft fleet would grow significantly.

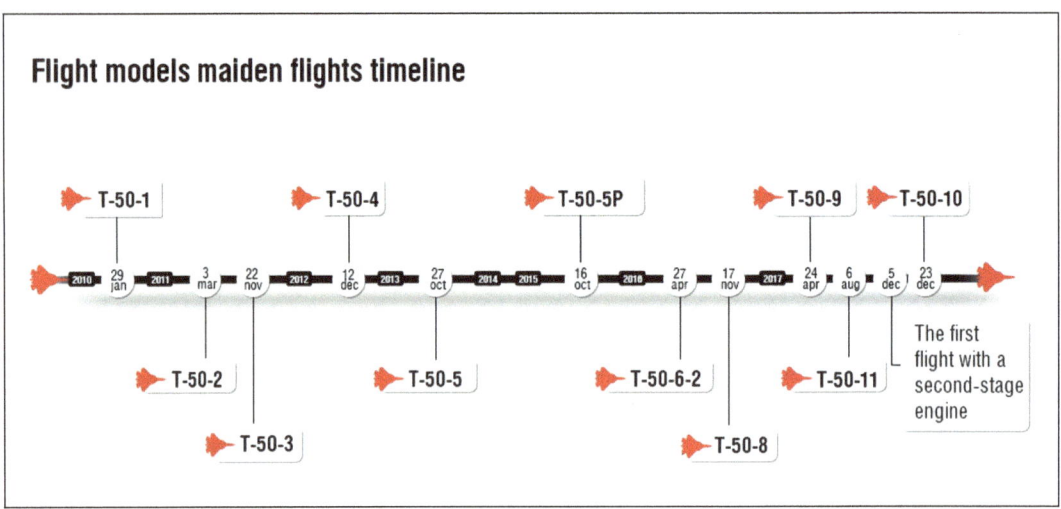

Top: Following a landing accident, T-50-5 was repaired and re-joined the test fleet as the T-50-5P. Bottom: Chart detailing maiden flight dates of the respective flight test models. MODRF/UAC-Sukhoi

Phase 1 of the official State Test Program was completed around December 2015. According to Viktor Bondarev, Commander in Chief of the VKS (Russian Aerospace Forces – the Russian Federation Air Force was absorbed into the Aerospace Forces on 1 August 2015), the T-50 was then to be put through a rigorous series of exercises and testing as soon as the pre-production aircraft were available. Under summer 2015 planning the first pre-production aircraft was scheduled for delivery in late 2016 or early 2017. These would be incorporated into a de-facto operational evaluation program within the Aerospace Forces. In the event, T-50-6-2 entered final assembly in early 2016 and conducted its maiden flight on 27 April that year, T-50-8 conducted its maiden flight on 17 November 2016, T-50-9 conducted its maiden flight on 24 April 2017, T-50-10 conducted its maiden flight on 23 December 2017 and T-50-11 conducted its maiden flight on 6 August 2017 (UAC) – as noted above, Victor Bondarev, the Commander in Chief of the Russian Aerospace Forces, revealed that the T-50 had been designated Su-57 in 2017. There was no development aircraft designated T-50-7 – the side code '057' was applied to a mock-up of the T-50 (Su-57/E).

The seventh flight test prototype/development T-50, T-50-8, during a test flight over an interior waterway. MODRF

Page 154-155. T-5-8 during a test flight, circa 20 August 2020. UAC

As the number of development/pre-production aircraft increased, development and service testing ramped up through the second half of the 2010's. An Su-57 development aircraft crashed during a test flight in the vicinity of Komsomolsk-on-Amur airfield on 24 December 2019, the pilot ejecting from the stricken aircraft safely. However, this low point in the development program was overshadowed by the highs, which had included the maiden flight of an Su-57, T-50-2, powered by a Stage Two engine on 5 December 2017, when Sergey Bogdan took the aircraft aloft from the Gromov Flight Research Institute on a 17 minute flight (UAC).

Su-57

Page 156 top: T-50-9 on a development flight in environmental conditions of snow/ice. Page 156 bottom-page 158: In 2017, T-50-2 was configured as the Product 30 Stage Two engine testbed with a single unit installed in the port engine bay, retaining an AL-41F1 turbofan in the starboard engine bay. The aircraft flew in this configuration for the first time on 5 December 2017. UAC

Top: T-50-1 was fitted with a non-standard extension at the extremity of the rear fuselage. Bottom: The last of the development/pre-series T-50 aircraft, T-50-11, was the second last to attain flight status when it conducted its maiden flight on 6 August 2017, more than four months prior to the maiden flight of T-50-10. Rostec/UAC

Su-57

Page 160-161: Series of photographs of quartets of T-50 (Su-57) development/pre-series aircraft during flight testing. MODRF

T-50 development aircraft during flight testing. UAC/Sukhoi

T-50 development aircraft, T-50-2 (fore) and T-50-1 (aft) during flight testing. UAC

Top: Two T-50 aircraft, T-50-2 (foreground) and T-50-4 (background) hold as they wait for take-off for a development flight. Above: T-50 flight testing demonstrated the designs excellent handling and flight characteristics. MODRF/UAC

By the close of 2017, UAC/Sukhoi had confirmed that development tests, then being conducted on nine flight test aircraft and various ground based test articles, had shown the design possessed 'good stability and handling performance' in subsonic and supersonic flight regimes, at low and upper altitudes and at the full range of angles of attack out to the post stall regime (Sukhoi/UAC). The design had also shown good control during flight refueling and when configured with differential fuel-stores loads. The focus of flight testing then fell on refining 'combat system-operating modes, interfacing with weapons, and the use of weapons' (UAC/Sukhoi). This also included operating with other platforms, including uninhabited aircraft (drones). To this end, the first joint test flight with a Su-57 (T-50) and an S-70 Okhotnik uninhabited aircraft lasted around 30 minutes. This basic flight test involved various interactions between the Su-57 and the Okhotnik, and initial detection of and designation of targets for the drone by the Su-57 onboard radar complex.

Page 165-166: The Su-57 conducted flight development tests operating with the S-70 Okhotnik uninhabited strike aircraft. Current (2021) planning envisioned a single Su-57 controlling up to four Okhotnik drones in a strike package. Sukhoi/MODRF

Dense vapour layer forms on the upper surface of T-50 aircraft manoeuvring during a development testing. Rostec

Page 168-170: T-50-4. MODRF/UAC

The T-50 (Su-57) had been designed and developed by PJSC Sukhoi as lead contractor, serial aircraft would be built at Knaaz *them*, Gagarin, both subsidiaries of UAC. The first serial produced Su-57 was delivered to a regiment of the Russian Aerospace Forces in the Southern Military District on 25 December 2020. By that time it was clear that the design had demonstrated exceptional flight performance in the horizontal and vertical flight regimes at speed ranges from low subsonic up to beyond Mach 2. The Su-57 had also underwent testing in an operational environment in two separate deployments to the Syrian Arab Republic from 2018. The first deployment, lasting two days, was conducted with two pre-series development aircraft. The second deployment involved operations with new types of bombs and missiles cleared for use by the Su-57.

Top: An Su-57 prepares to take-off from Hmeymim air base during a deployment to Syria. Bottom: An Su-57 with spoof paint scheme mimicking a smaller forward canard-delta configuration. MODRF

Su-57

Page 172-175: T-50-8 is demonstrated at the Army-2020 International Military Technical Forum, circa 27 August 2020. UAC

Assembly of serial Su-57 aircraft on the occasion of Russian Defence Minister visit to the Knaaz production line at Komsomolsk-on-Amur, circa 12 August 2020. MODRF

Su-57

Page 177-179: Serial produced Su-57 in the assembly hall, roll-out to proceed to the paint shop and maiden flight. UAC

Around this time the program was moving from development toward serial production. To this end, a contract was signed between the MODRF (Ministry of Defence of the Russian Federation) and PJSC Sukhoi at the Army Forum 2018, on 22 August that year. This covered the delivery of two Su-57 aircraft to the MODRF Aerospace Forces. At the Army Forum the following year, a contract was signed covering the delivery of 76 Su-57 aircraft to the Russian Aerospace Forces. Initial uncertainty about whether or not this equated to 2+76 or 2+74 for a total of 76 was clarified in 2020. In late August that year, Rostec Corporation confirmed that ORPE Obninsk Technologiya would produce 74 sets of Polymer composite materials for the construction of serial Su-57 aircraft (Rostec). This effectively confirmed that the total of 76 Su-57 ordered included the two aircraft previously contracted for, the composite materials of which had been contracted for separately.

The first serial produced Su-57 was delivered to a regiment of the Russian Aerospace Forces in the Southern Military District on 25 December 2020. Planning called for delivery of four more Su-57 aircraft during the course of 2021, with a total of 22 such aircraft scheduled to be delivered by the close of 2024. The first serial produced Su-57 powered by the Product 30 Second Stage engine was scheduled to be assembled in 2022, and all 76 Su-57's under contract were scheduled to be delivered to the Aerospace Forces by the end of 2028 (TASS) – planning in 2020 called for production to eventually reach around 15 aircraft per year.

From 2025, planning (as at summer 2021) called for production to move to an updated variant of the Su-57 developed under the Magapolis research and development program. Although confirmed details were sparse in 2021, this was expected to introduce a more advanced cockpit with enhanced capability avionics systems, and would also incorporate the aforementioned Second Stage engines (TASS). The Magapolis program was also apparently the vehicle for design of a two-seat variant of the Su-57, although it was unclear, in 2021, whether such an aircraft would be aimed solely at potential export operators or if it would be procured by the Russian Aerospace Forces. The Russian Deputy Defence Minister had stated prior that it would be developed in an export configuration (TASS). One role mooted for such an aircraft was the control of swarms of Okhotnik uninhabited strike drones. It was confirmed that the baseline single-seat Su-57 being delivered to the Russian Aerospace Forces would be capable of controlling a quartet of Okhotnik drones (capable of conducting air to air and air to ground/surface roles), work continuing in this direction in 2021.

Page 180: Model of T-50 (Su-57) derivative at the Bangalore air show (undated). Page 181: Model of T-50 (Su-57) derivative at Aero India 2021. Sukhoi/UAC

Under 2021 planning, the baseline serial Su-57 may become a model for a family of combat aircraft derivatives in the mold of its fourth generation Su-27 forebear (Yuri Slyusar, General Director, UAC). Variations would be aimed at potential export orders as well as further potential domestic orders. An export variant, designated Su-57E, was presented at the MAKS-2019 trade exhibition. Two years later, at MAKS-2021 in July that year, Rosoboronexport confirmed that it was in negotiations with five countries over potential sales of the Su-57E (TASS 20 July 2021), the previous month it being intimated that the five countries were in the South East Asia region (TASS, 16 June 2021). The Su-57 had become a focus of export interest over the previous year or so, having been authorised for export in summer 2020, with a full-scale model of the export standard Su-57E exhibited at the Aero India show in February 2021 (TASS, 1 February, 2021).

India had long been associated with the T-50 PAK FA program under the Indo-Russian FGFA program. By late 2001, India had increasingly become associated with the Russian LFI ((*Legikiy Frontovoi Istrebitel* – Light Frontline Fighter) program even though no formal agreement had been entered into. It was clear that India would be in the market for an advanced fifth generation fighter aircraft design. That nation's aviation industry ties with the Russian aviation industry, already established, but firmly cemented with the Su-30MKI 4th+ generation super-manoeuvrable multifunctional fighter program, paved the way for further cooperation on a future fighter program. Tacit understanding on joint development of a fifth generation fighter aircraft for India was reached towards the end of 2001 (Harkins, 2015).

On 18 October 2007, an agreement on joint development and production of a fifth generation fighter aircraft for the IAF (Indian Air Force) was signed in Moscow under the auspices of the 7th Session of the Russian-Indian Intergovernmental commission on military-technical cooperation. On 21 December 2010, agreement was reached on conceptual and technical design work for the new fighter design, involving Russian Rosoboronexport companies and HAL (Hindustan Aeronautics Limited) in India. During the Russian President's visit to India, details emerged of the agreement between Rosoboronexport, Sukhoi and HAL on the preliminary design and development for the FGFA multifunctional fighter for the IAF, which would use the T-50 as its basis. The agreement called for design of a two-seat variant and a more powerful fifth generation engine. At the Bangalore Air show in India in early 2013, Sukhoi exhibited a model of the FGFA adorned in Indian Air Force colours (Harkins, 2015).

In October 2011, India had announced a requirement for 214 fifth generation multifunctional fighter aircraft, consisting of 166 single-seat and 48 two-seat aircraft. Overly optimistic, the IAF stated that it expected to take deliveries of the first aircraft in 2017. In 2012, the then Chief of Staff of the IAF, Air Marshal Norman Anil Kumar Browne, stated that the number of aircraft to be procured had been reduced to 144, all of which were to be single-seat aircraft, the two-seat variant being dropped in order to reduce program development costs. Potential deliveries of the aircraft to India had also been put back to 2020 (Harkins, 2015). In 2021, the direction of India's future fifth generation fighter remains undecided with no formal order placed.

A quartet of Su-57 development aircraft overfly Red Square, Moscow, during the Victory Day parade on 9 May 2020. UAC

Su-57

Page 183 top: A trio of Su-57 development aircraft during a demonstration. Page 183 bottom-page 184: Su-57 aircraft during the rehearsal for the Victory Day parade on 6 May 2021. Sukhoi/UAC

The first T-50 (Su-57) development aircraft, T-50-1 (top), and the third flight development aircraft, T-50-3 (bottom). Sukhoi/UAC

The fifth development Su-57, T-50-5/T-50-5P. UAC/Sukhoi

Two ship formations of T-50 development/pre-series aircraft during the state flight test program. MODRF

T-50 development aircraft T-50-1 – T-50-5				
Aircraft	Code	First Flight	Pilot	Duration
T-50-1	051	29 January 2010	Sergey Bogdan	47 minutes
T-50-2	052	3 March 2011	Sergey Bogdan	44 minutes
T-50-3	053	22 November 2011	Sergey Bogdan	Just over 1 hour
T-50-4	054	12 December 2012	Sergey Bogdan	40 minutes
T-50-5	055	27 October 2013	Roman Kondratyev	50 minutes

Extended T-50 (Su-57) prototype development and pre-series development aircraft		
Aircraft	Maiden Flight	Code
T-50-1	29 January 2010	
T-50-2	3 March 2011	
T-50-3	22 November 2011	
T-50-4	12 December 2012	
T-50-5	27 October 2013	
T-50-5P	16 October 2015	
T-50-6-2	27 April 2016	
T-50-8	17 November 2016	
T-50-9	24 April 2017	
T-50-10	23 December 2017	
T-50-11	6 August 2017	
T-50-2 with Stage 2 engine	5 December 2017	
There was no T-50-7, but the side code '057' was applied to a mock-up of the T-50		

Fourth development T-50, T-50-4. KnAAPO

Serial Su-57. UAC

Top: T-50-1. Bottom: A T-50 (Su-57) development/pre-series aircraft climbs during a demonstration at the Army-2021 exhibition on 24 August 2021. UAC

A Su-57 climbs out on a development/test flight silhouetted against the Sun, circa 16 July 2021. UAC

Top: Four ship formation of T-50 aircraft during the state flight test program. As the sun sets on the initial T-50 development clearance for the Su-57 it rose on the service entry of the latter to service with the Russian Aerospace Forces. MODRF/Sukhoi

GLOSSARY

AFAR	Active-Phased Array Radar
APAR	Active Phased Array Radar
ATF	Advanced Tactical Fighter
AWACS	Airborne Warning and Control System
ECM	Electronic Counter Measures
FCS	Flight Control System
FGFA	Fifth Generation Fighter Aircraft
g	Gravity (1 g = 1 times Earth gravity)
GLONASS	Globanaya Navigozionnaya Sputnikovaya Sistema (Global Navigation Satellite System)
GosNIIAS	Federal State Unitary Enterprise State Research Centre of Aviation Systems
GRPZ	State Ryazan Instrument Plant
HAL	Hindustan Aeronautics Limited
HMTS	Helmet Mounted Targeting System
HOTAS	Hands-On Throttle and Stick
HUD	Heads Up Display
IAF	Indian Air Force
IMS	Information Management System
kg	Kilogram
kgf	Kilogram Force
km/h	Kilometers per Hour
KnAAPO	Komsomolsk-on-Amur Aircraft Production Association
Knaaz	Komsomolsk-on-Amur Aviation Plant, named after Yu.A Gagarin
KNIRTI	Kaluga Research Radio Engineering Institute
LDIRCM	Laser Directed Infrared Counter Measures
LFI	*Legikiy Frontovoi Istrebitel* – Light Frontline Fighter
m	Meter
Mach	1 Mach = the speed of sound (this varies with altitude)
MAPO	Moscow Aircraft Production Association
MFI	Mnogofunktsional'nyy Frontovoi Istrebitel – Multifunctional Frontline Fighter
MiG	Mikoyan
MODRF	Ministry Of Defence of the Russian Federation
NATO	North Atlantic Treaty Organisation
OLS	Optical Location Station
PAK DA	*Perspektivniy Aviacionniy Complex Bol'shaya Dal'nost* – Perspective Aviation Complex for Long Range Aviation
PAK FA	*Perspektivniy Aviacionniy Complex Frontovoi Aviacii* – Perspective Aviation Complex for Frontline Aviation
RAC	Russian Aircraft Corporation
RCS	Radar Cross Section

Su	Sukhoi
TASS	Russian News Agency
TMC	Tactical Missiles Corporation
TsAGI	Central Hydrodynamic Institute, named after Z.E. Zhukovsky
UAC	United Aircraft Corporation
UEC	United Engine Corporation
UEIA	Ufa (Engine) Industrial Association
UHF	Ultra-High Frequency
UMPO	Ufa-based Motor Building Association
USAF	United States Air Force
VHF	Very High Frequency
VKS	Russian Aerospace Defense Forces (Russian Federation Air Force)
x	Times (multiplication)
°	Degree(s)
±	Plus or minus
~	Approximately equal to (can also be used to mean asymptotically equal)

ABOUT THE AUTHOR

Hugh Harkins FRAS, MIstP, MRAeS is a physicist/historian and author with an extensive research/study background in aeronautic, astronautic, astrophysics, geophysics, nautical and the wider scientific, technical and historical fields. He is also involved in research in the field of Scottish history, which formed an element of dual undergraduate degrees. Hugh has published in excess of sixty books, non-fiction and fiction, writing under his given name as well as utilising several pseudonyms. He has also written for several international magazines, whilst his work has been used as reference for many other projects, ranging from the aviation industry, international news corporations and film media to encyclopaedias, museum exhibits and the computer gaming industry. Hugh is an elected member of the Institute of Physics and Royal Aeronautical Society and is an elected Fellow of the Royal Astronomical Society. He currently resides in his native Scotland. Other titles by the author include:

Air War over Syria, Tu-160, Tu-95MS & Tu-22M3 - Cruise Missile and Bombing Strikes on Syria, November 2015-February 2016
Sukhoi T-50/PAK FA - Russia's 5th Generation 'Stealth' Fighter
Su-34 – Russia's 4th+ Generation Strike Fighter
Sukhoi Su-35S 'Flanker' E - Russia's 4++ Generation Super-Manoeuvrability Fighter
Sukhoi Su-30MKK/MK2/M2 - Russo Kitayshiy Striker from Amur
MiG-35/D 'Fulcrum' F – Towards the Fifth Generation
Sukhoi Su-27SM(3)/SKM
Yak-130 – Advanced Trainer/Light Combat Aircraft
Su-33 – Russia's Carrier-Borne Strike Fighter
Dassault Rafale, The Gallic Squall
Nimrod MRA4 – Demise of the Mighty Hunter
Russian/Soviet Aircraft Carrier & Carrier Aviation Design & Evolution Volume 1 - Seaplane Carriers, Project 71/72, Graf Zeppelin, Project 1123 ASW Cruiser & Project 1143-1143.4 Heavy Aircraft Carrying Cruiser
Soviet Mixed Power Experimental Fighter Aircraft – Piston-Liquid Propellant Rocket Engine/Piston-Ramjet/Piston-Pulsejet & Piston-Compressor Jet Engine Designs of the 1940's
Russian/Soviet Submarine Launched Ballistic Missiles: Nuclear Deterrence/Counter Force Strike
Russia's Strategic Missile Carrier/Bomber Roadmap 2018-2040 – PAK DA, Tu-160M2, Tu-95MSM & Tu-22M3M
Russia's Coastal Missile Shield - Bal-E & Bastion Mobile Coastal Cruise Missile Complexes
Iskander - Mobile Tactical Aero-Ballistic/Cruise Missile Complex
Orbital/Fractional Orbit Bombardment System - The Soviet Globalnaya Raketa
Counter-Space Defence Co-Orbital Satellite Fighter
Raid on the Forth - The First German Air Raid on Great Britain in World War II
Light Battle Cruisers and the Second Battle of Heligoland Bight
X-35 - Progenitor to the F-35 Lightning II
X-32 - The Boeing Joint Strike Fighter
Boeing X-36 Tailless Agility Flight Research Aircraft
XF-103 – Mach 3 Stratospheric Interceptor Concept
North American F-108 Rapier - Mach 3 Interceptor
Convair YB-60 - Fort Worth Overcast
Into The Cauldron - The Lancaster MK.I Daylight Raid on Augsburg
Hurricane IIB Combat Log - 151 Wing RAF, North Russia 1941
RAF Meteor Jet Fighters in World War II, an Operational Log
Typhoon IA/B Combat Log - Operation Jubilee, August 1942

www.ingramcontent.com/pod-product-compliance
Lightning Source LLC
Chambersburg PA
CBHW041949240426
43668CB00035B/34